WE'RE POTTY TRAINING!

The First-Time Dad's Potty-Training Survival Guide

ADRIAN KULP

ILLUSTRATIONS BY JEREMY NGUYEN

ROCKRIDGE
PRESS

Series Designer: Antonio Valverde
Interior and Cover Designer: Heather Krakora
Art Producer: Sue Bischofberger
Editor: Mo Mozuch
Production Editor: Jenna Dutton
Production Manager: Holly Haydash

Illustrations © 2021 Jeremy Nguyen

ISBN: Print 978-1-64876-563-6 | eBook 978-1-64876-564-3
R0

To my kids—
Ava, Charlie, Mason, and Evelyn.
I'm not afraid to reverse-engineer
this book when it comes time for
you to wipe my ass . . .

Contents

INTRODUCTION

For those of you who perhaps haven't read some of my previous books or haven't followed the award-nominated parenting blog that I started over a decade ago, my name is Adrian Kulp, but I'm better known in the parenting circles as @Dad_or_Alive.

I spent close to 15 years as a comedy executive for the likes of Adam Sandler, Chelsea Handler, David Letterman, and Craig Ferguson at *The Late Late Show* on CBS. I developed and produced all kinds of comedy, stand-up, and television, but never in a million years did I think writing bathroom humor might eventually come full circle and turn back to find me in a literal fashion.

In 2009, my wife and I were blessed with the first of our four children, Ava. (In the following nine years, we quickly added two boys and another girl: Charlie, Mason, and Evelyn.) After I left my role as a comedy executive in 2010, my wife went back to her full-time executive position in unscripted television (those are fancy words for trashy reality TV). This was the moment, as a first-time father, that the training wheels came off and I became a full-time, stay-at-home dad. There was no one to test the temperature of breast milk before feeding, give me advice on sleep habits, or be the extra hand to toss me a wipe during a public blowout. There were many books out there, but they were predominantly written by women, for women.

So I started a blog, *Dad or Alive*. In 2018, I penned *We're Parents! The First-Time Pregnancy Handbook*, a best-seller since its debut. I've since worked with hundreds of parenting brands, spoken at numerous parenting and fatherhood conferences, and published five more books—including the latest one you're holding—because I felt obligated to share some of the knowledge and tools I've picked up along the way.

Before potty training, I was changing diapers. That first diaper change happened at Cedars-Sinai hospital in Los Angeles, with my wife, parents, and in-laws standing around. To my own embarrassment, I didn't know that girls needed to be wiped from front to back. How would I know that? I never had any sisters growing up, only brothers. I almost never babysat. And most of my girlfriends in college used the bathroom with the door closed. I guess I somehow missed the page devoted to that action in all those overwhelming expectant-parent paperbacks.

After mastering diaper changing, I was called on to master potty training. Potty training usually doesn't just happen on its own and it's a milestone for both the child AND the parent. It's truly one of the first times that you see your child learn cause-and-effect.

The goal of this handbook is to help you navigate the ins and outs of potty training and design a tailored plan with an easy, multistep process.

This book includes practical tips, tools, and advice to equip you with the best possible potty-training knowledge. The book is in four parts, consisting of seven chapters in all. These chapters will take you from start to finish: identifying when it's the right time to begin, a toolkit to help you gear up (emotionally and physically), and tactics and advice on the how-to that will hopefully help you WANT to conquer potty training.

Even if you're one of the lucky ones and potty training comes without many obstacles, there are often regressions or unexpected challenges later. If that happens, or if you're truly unsure how to provide the best care for your child, I encourage you to seek professional help from your pediatrician or primary-care physician.

Additionally, any ongoing or debilitating feelings of depression, anxiety, and other mental health issues (for you or your child) should be addressed by a medical professional. This book isn't meant as a replacement for a therapist, medication, or medical treatment. There is no shame in seeking treatment or additional help!

With that said, this is your chance to experience diaper freedom. No more freezing-your-ass-off December diaper triage stations set up in the back of your SUV while other shoppers drive by and stare. Say goodbye to forgetting to pack enough diapers on your weekend trip to Nana's and just think about that cold hard CASH you'll be saving every week.

Not just that, but it's also a chance to face your fears about potty training, commit to the process no matter the challenges, and think of it as an opportunity to bond with your child. I'm gonna help you get there.

PART I

WELCOME TO POTTY TRAINING

Not every child is going to come charging down the stairs like William Wallace in *Braveheart* with their faces painted, demanding their diaper freedom. I wish it would've been that easy for me (with one of my offspring, it actually was, but more on that later). That's why we have this first chapter, to talk about when starting might be a good idea. We'll discuss a few of the telltale physical and developmental signs, communication tips, and what to do if siblings are part of the mix.

CHAPTER 1

Potty Training as a First-Time Dad

In this chapter, we'll talk all about assessing the "right" time to start potty training and some of the most common signs that your child is telling you that they're ready to go.

Welcome to the Wild World of Potty Training

As a first-time dad and one who also stayed at home as a primary caregiver for several years, I had to get my game up to speed pretty quickly. It often felt that as soon as I had a routine down or understood a certain level of development, everything would change, JUST LIKE THAT. Kids mature at such a rapid rate that there was no time to become comfortable.

At the time, a lot of our friends also had kids around the same age. What no one tells you is that once you have kids, you start to collect couples who have kids the same ages, whether you're an extrovert like my wife (and think this is awesome), or an introvert like me (my one friend is just fine, thank you!). While that sounds wonderful in theory—we commiserated, traded battle stories, and had many laughs with one another—it also created a subtle bubble of competition.

"Little Jimmy is just crushing it with using the potty: straight shooter, no splash; it's insane! He's gotta be a genius. Because of this, we may start him in pre-K right now!"

"What in the hell," I would ask. "What's Jimmy got going on that my kid doesn't have?" TIME TO RAMP IT UP . . . and therein was my first mistake.

There Is No Right Time to Start

Let's just go on record here: Between the two of us, my wife is in the "I want them to be little as long as possible" camp, while I sit squarely on team "Diapers = big money." With our first toddler, my wife and I debated for weeks over when the right time to start might be. We considered the fact that I was at home, so I could devote more time with fewer interruptions to make sure it all happened successfully. However, we also considered weekend trips or mini vacations we planned and thought about how much of a pain potty training would be while tackling serious road miles or a theme park in the summer.

So, there is no right time to start. You take the cues that your kids are giving you and run with it.

Average Age for Potty Training

If there's one certainty in the potty-training journey, it's that every child is developing on their own timeline. As long as you're within established parameters and your pediatrician isn't concerned, you're doing fine.

In the United States, children generally are ready for potty training between 18 and 24 months. Many kids find success in daytime training by the age of two. Some might not actually be ready to train until they're closer to the age of three.

Although some parents may be a bit antsy to drop the diaper habit early, studies show that children under 18 months of age don't usually have the necessary bladder or bowel control. Toddlers under 18 months also do not yet have a true understanding of cause and effect, a concept that is helpful in training.

WHAT IF YOUR CHILD IS POTTY TRAINED BEFORE OR AFTER OTHER KIDS?

We've been fortunate to have enough space between the birth of our children that potty training largely resembled a line of dominoes falling in succession (though at one point one of our boys surpassed the other in nighttime potty training). Our older children have always served as positive learning examples for their younger siblings by allowing them to watch as they went about doing it themselves. Parents shouldn't get worried if a younger sibling surpasses an older one when it comes to the process—you may need to encourage that younger sibling and reinforce the idea that there shouldn't be any teasing or over-the-top bragging about their success.

With peers, don't sweat it if other kids are beating your son or daughter to the finish line. Everyone moves at a different pace. Plus, from a child's perspective, having peers that are further advanced can serve as a positive example during playdates.

Watch for Signs Your Child Is Ready

There are definitely physical signs that you can look for as your child begins to get near that 18-month-old mark. I've listed several below. You might also spot your child watching as you go to the bathroom; playing with their dolls or toys and making them use the potty; or going into the bathroom and making attempts to pull their pants down.

Pulling at a Wet or Dirty Diaper

One of those images that consistently haunts me is being over at a friend's house with their kid walking around with a hundred pounds of urine in their diaper. My internal dialogue went something like, "What is this dude waiting for? A full-on UTI or to see if it can actually get so heavy that it scrapes the ground as they walk?"

At a certain point, a lot of children will be the first ones to make parents aware that they've gone to the bathroom. An overwhelming disdain for soiled diapers is a good sign that your child might be ready to give potty training a shot.

Hiding to Pee or Poop

No, I'm not talking about kids hiding logs around the house like Easter eggs, but hiding themselves. When the inner stress prompted by your child's normal development kicks in, they might go behind the sofa or inside the pantry to "cop a squat," as my Southern family says. When you find them hiding in the corner or in their playpen with a diaper that is warm to the touch (due to a recent pee or poop), this could be a strong sign that they're ready to begin potty training.

Having a Dry Diaper for Longer than Usual

Two of my children were both able to make it through the night in a dry diaper before potty training, which left my wife and me astonished. We wondered if somehow they were dehydrated. Technically, my son was born with three kidneys and an adult-sized bladder, which essentially meant that he had cheated potty training, but it was still impressive to see this happen. That was the impetus for us to consider making the jump away from diapers. In a normal scenario, a toddler who consistently has a dry diaper more than likely is demonstrating a mastering of bladder control so is ready to try potty training.

Dexterity and Overall Motor Skills

Noticing your child's ability to perform somewhat simple motor functions, such as pulling up or pushing down their own pants, is a checkmark in the "positive" column. Also, the ability to stay seated for more than 10 seconds qualifies as another plus (this can sometimes also be achieved with the aid of a book or tablet). Hope you like listening to potty songs on YouTube!

INSIDE YOUR CHILD'S MIND

Your toddler is a sponge, soaking up everything they see and hear (which is why I should probably binge *Ozark* after they've already gone to bed instead of during dinner prep; my bad). So, they're probably watching you and your partner use the bathroom from time to time and wondering where Mom's or Dad's diapers are. You don't have to tell them about college pledge pranks, but talk to them about how big kids and grown-ups wear underpants. Just discussing it, and asking if they'd like to pick some out, might get your little one's mind moving in that direction.

Just as There Is No Right Time to Start, There Is No Specific Timeline

We know that a parent's job is to gently push their kids into new and daunting life stages, but in all honesty, where potty training is concerned, the best thing you can do for your child is to NOT push them into transitioning out of diapers before they're ready. Doing so will not only put unnecessary stress on them (which could eventually lead to regressions) but will also challenge your own patience (that patience that I wasn't born with!). Like most things that result in success, staying patient and consistent are of paramount importance. If you regress, they'll likely regress. This is no time to get lazy.

The thing about potty training (full potty training: pee and poop, whether it be daytime, naptime, or nighttime) is that you really have no idea how long it might take. Most estimates come in between three and six months of training; however, there are certainly instances when it's taken much less time or considerably more. We have four kids, and two of them landed well beyond each end of this estimate.

Some Kids Take Days, Some Weeks, Some Months, and Some ... Years

Attempting to start potty training before your child is ready could lead to a much more frustrating—and much longer—process.

You could always have the complete anomaly the way we did with our fourth baby, Evelyn. At 22 months, she showed us that she wanted to use the potty. We pulled out the small potty that we'd had for 10 years and three kids, fully preparing ourselves with training diapers and swim diapers and nighttime diapers, and being ready for A BATTLE, and much to our surprise, she never turned back. Neither of us knew that day that we had changed our very last diaper.

On the flip side of the coin, potty training for the daytime is much different from getting through the night. This process could take not just months, but sometimes, as in the case of our first and second children, years.

Most kids are potty-trained by the age of five or six.

Many parents who haven't gone through potty training or haven't done any research before attempting it may just see it as a one-and-done thing. There are actually a few steps within the process and keeping up the communication between you, other caregivers, and your children is imperative. Pee training is the act of successfully getting your child to sit down and pee. Poop training is the act of getting them to not only sit down and pee, but also poop—which not all kids will do. Once you've mastered those two, then you've got boys standing up to pee, making it through naptime, and the hardest of all, making it through the night. Remember to offer positive reinforcement to your kids on every little achievement. It will help build their self-confidence and hopefully bring you closer to the finish line.

It Also Depends on Your Child's Personality

Let's be real for a second: Potty training is one of those basic, albeit messy, developmental processes that you AREN'T GOING TO MESS UP. You just aren't. You've probably never met a teenager who has gone to college wearing diapers. Unless they're part of the Greek system, and then that's just a whole different story (not sure why I keep mentioning that; PTSD perhaps).

Just keep in mind that it WILL eventually work. But there are a lot of variables that contribute to the success, or lack thereof, in potty training, and one of the biggest is personality. There are diaper brands and influencers that have really built thoughtful forums, campaigns, and discussions around "potty personalities." The websites for Pull-Ups and Pampers, along with destinations like "What to Expect" and Parents.com, offer some valuable insights into the peaks and valleys of potty training.

Some of the most common personalities are:

- ▶ INTROVERT AND STRONG-WILLED: These two personality traits seem to ride together. Many introverted children will seem shy and reluctant to change. They may take some warming up to new situations.
- ▶ EXTROVERT: This personality is generally excited and ready to go. They're outgoing and overtly expressive. They just need to nail down the routine and you're off to the races.
- ▶ EASYGOING/LAID BACK/PATIENT: This personality sounds like someone I would want to hang out with, but alas, when dealing with toddlers and toilets, kids with this trait will need a lot of attention and encouragement to concentrate on detail. Games might be the perfect way to get them from point A to point B.

▶ **SENSITIVE AND INTUITIVE:** These types of children are focused, determined, and somewhat predictable. They pay close attention to the rules that you've established and can sometimes be borderline obsessive. They may also like to be very "clean."

Like Everything Else, Potty Training is an Adventure

If you're someone who enjoys the luxury of planning things out and adhering to a specific roadmap before embarking on an adventure, potty training could be the detour that you weren't expecting.

Not only do you have to navigate finding the right time to start and HOW to start (more on that in chapter 3), you need to help your child know when to go.

And if we're talking about this as if it's a journey (and it is), we've only packed our bags and gotten in the truck. Now we've got to actually turn the truck on and figure out which roads are easiest when it comes to different sexes; transitioning to big-kid underwear; potty training away from home and at night; and dealing with regression that will likely happen. There'll be curves in the road for sure, but the destination will always be worth it.

There May Be Starts and Stops Along the Way

Don't get down on yourself if you reach a point at which you need to stop potty training. With at least one of our kids, we had started the process, then had a road trip or vacation that impeded the process.

Whether it's something similar or you just made a miscalculation on whether or not you or your child was ready, know that these things happen. Whether or not you misread your child's signals, they're fearful, or they just don't want any part of it, if you're within the recommended age range, then you shouldn't worry about it. Exercise patience, pull back, regroup, and get back into it, maybe in a few weeks, when the timing seems right—for THEM, not necessarily for you.

How Will You Know When You're Ready?

Knowing when your child is ready to start potty training ends up being a combination of physical and behavioral clues that you collect along the way. If your child is demonstrating actions like grunting, hiding, and squatting in corners, or "pushing" until they're red in the face, they're physiologically ready. If your child's dexterity and motor skills show that they're able to perform simple functions like pulling down their pants and/or pulling them up, coupled with sitting for several minutes at a time, you've put a checkmark in the "ready" column. Being able to verbally express themselves (i.e., "I've gotta go potty") is gravy on the mashed potatoes.

How Do I Manage My Anxiety as a First-Time Dad?

There's nothing more daunting than trying something for the first time. There's RISK, but also REWARD in this action. Yes, you could find yourself in a position of failure. With our first child, I thought I had potty training mastered. After a week or two of allowing my daughter to roam naked throughout the house while following her around and asking her every 20 minutes if she needed to use the potty, I felt confident in the idea that I might be able to make a simple grocery run (clothing not optional, of course).

I had her use the potty before leaving. I had my grocery list organized by aisle to maximize my effectiveness. My downfall was the slowest deli worker that I've ever encountered. With a full cart, I was only a few steps from the finish line. But while we waited, my daughter peed in her pants. I had to seek out the manager and have an employee come out with a mop after the intercom clicked on with "Cleanup in the deli; cleanup in the deli." Navigating my cart around a series of "wet floor" cones was a stinging reminder that potty training has its ups and downs.

Remind yourself that every parent has been through this and made mistakes. Messes happen, but cleanups are always possible. Stay calm and exercise patience—this isn't the end of the world.

FINDING THE RIGHT TIME

My wife and I always struggled to find the right time to begin potty training. Life is easier changing a diaper every once in a while. But having to be on your toes, hovering around your child nonstop for a week (or more) and being on the lookout for random puddles and droppings takes courage and commitment.

Many of you likely can't or don't want to take off work for a week to potty train. So how do you string together enough days for this thing to have a chance of clicking? Consider holiday weekends that you might be able to bookend with sick (don't tell your boss) days.

If you have to hand a partially potty-trained toddler over to another caregiver, daycare, or childcare, give them a written update on your plan and approach and see if they can bring it home!

Potty-Training FAQ

Parenting is already full of questions, and potty training even more so. Here are some of the questions you've probably been thinking about and some answers that might surprise you.

Are girls easier to potty train than boys?

One of the most common myths about potty training is that girls have quicker success than boys; however, that's not always the case—one shouldn't get overconfident.

Will pull-ups make training take longer?

Another common myth is that the use of pull-ups can prolong the potty-training process, while the reality, more often than not, is that they serve as a crucial transitional tool for children.

How do I prepare my child for potty training?

I've devoted an entire section of this book to help mentally and physically prepare your child AND yourself for this journey (see chapter 3 on page 45).

What happens if I try to potty train too early and it doesn't work?

It's not a loss if you realize that you may have tried to potty train too early. Stay positive, pull back, and before starting, wait a few weeks to see if your child has an increased interest.

What should I do about my child wetting the bed during nap-time or nighttime?

Accidents will definitely happen. Limiting fluids and waking kids up to go to the bathroom are among the most common tricks, which we cover in chapter 6 (see page 105).

What kinds of stuff will I need to get started?

It's totally possible to get started right away and toss your child on top of an adult-sized potty, but chances are that might just be too intimidating. I'd suggest looking for a kid-sized toilet that sits on the floor in close proximity to your own toilet, OR some type of insert that sits over your adult seat or clips in, plus a stepstool. We're going to cover this in the next chapter.

Wipes, plastic sheets, and a reward chart or little prizes might also be things to consider.

CHEAT SHEET

I'm all about reading the CliffsNotes if I have a test coming up, so here are the chapter's five key takeaways to make you look smart at your next parents' happy hour:

1. **THERE IS NO RIGHT TIME TO START POTTY TRAINING.** However, try to watch for signs and clues that can lead you as close as you can get to the right time. Confused yet?

2. **DON'T CREATE A TIMELINE IN YOUR HEAD FOR ACHIEVING DIAPER FREEDOM.** This could take one day or one year. Much like everything else in parenting, you have very little actual control, and the sooner you realize this, the happier you and your child will be.

3. **IDENTIFY YOUR CHILD'S "POTTY PERSONALITY."** This will help determine your approach.

4. **PATIENCE.** The capacity to accept or tolerate delay, problems, or suffering without getting angry or upset is crucial.

5. **DON'T ALLOW THE FEAR OF FAILURE TO CONTROL YOUR MINDSET.**

Conclusion

Every plan starts with a solid foundation. Hopefully I've given you the tools in this first chapter to identify your child's personality and recognize those signals that your child may be ready to begin the potty-training journey.

Next up we'll look at getting yourself and your partner into the appropriate headspace and the proper attitude. You've also got to get those people around you in agreement and be willing to seek out help and support when necessary.

CHAPTER 2

The Potty-Training Survival Toolkit

This chapter will explore how to find your confidence in potty training, as well as the best strategies for potty training with the help of everyone in your house, including caregivers and family members who may visit. We'll learn about consistency and the idea that waving the white flag and calling on the advice of a professional isn't considered a loss.

Get in the Right Mindset

Potty training isn't for the meek. You need to fully commit to knowing that this may or may NOT work out in everyone's favor right now. Success could be achieved overnight; however, it most likely will take weeks or potentially months. You need to be prepared for that journey.

Patience and persistence is the key to winning this battle. Stay calm and read on.

Your Child Will Know If You Aren't Confident

Fake it 'til you make it, Pops. Aside from finding your ability to be patient with potty training, the next trait you'll have to dig for is confidence. The bottom line is that no one wants to learn something from someone who doesn't seem like they know what they're doing. Even if you're on shifty footing with this, pretend.

Beyond this book, try to educate yourself as much as possible. Talk to friends who are parents and ask them about their experience with their kids. You'll quickly find a plethora of examples of what to do, what not to do, and, best of all, horror stories that you'll mentally bookmark and likely share with your partner or a friend about what to avoid. Take information in and file it away; at some point you'll realize that bits and pieces of the things you've heard along the way may help you and your child in the process. But as with everything having to do with parenting, opinions are varied, polarizing, and plentiful.

They Need You to Lead the Way

Admittedly, one of my "bad qualities" (insert my wife's voice here) is that I'm truly not great at follow-through. I love starting projects, but when I come up against serious adversity, I can lose the energy to course-correct, and end up backing down, never to make an attempt again. She also has told our therapist time and again that I am the King of Procrastination, and I suppose when you combine those two deadly sins in the same person, I could be perfectly happy stopping the potty training at the first accident, never to attempt again.

This clearly doesn't work when it comes to parenting, so I've had to really adjust my mentality when it comes to starting projects that aren't in my comfort zone. Similarly, you may find yourself wanting to stop and start this process time and again, but try not to. Persistence is absolutely pivotal here. Like any other parenting issue, the most important thing is to have your child see you work toward this goal alongside them, and not back down when the going gets tough.

That said, there's always the possibility that you get into potty training and the timing truly just isn't right for your child, and you DO need to step back and reassess. If you're already this far into this book because the developmental readiness signs have you nodding your head in agreement, then I think it's best to proceed.

Build Your Support Squad

Finding random "dad friends" for me at the playground is something that my wife has taken on as a side hobby after work or on the weekends, seemingly finding endless enjoyment in it. If you haven't yet been welcomed into the ninth circle of hell, the "man date" is a real thing in suburban mom circles. I can't tell you how many times she's come home saying:

> "Oh my gosh, I met this mom Rachel at the park today; she has two toddlers and a baby, and also an amaaaaaaaazing husband Chris and you're so much alike and he likes sports like you; he grills meat and does yardwork just like you. He also hates grapefruit AND he's from the East Coast like you and you'll just love him, so I made you a date to go out to lunch next Friday, so don't cancel, okay?"

Not everyone has family living close by, but there are lots of ways to build your social network. I don't officially recommend picking up friends randomly from the playground (though in this case my wife was right; Chris has become a part of our family over the years). But the truth is that even if you have a ton of friends and family nearby, having people who are going through the same things at the same time can be a life changer.

Sometimes your partner in commiseration comes in disguise. I'll never forget being a stay-at-home-dad and becoming friends with our mailman because he had a toddler at the same time I did. I found this out when he delivered the mail as I was pressure-washing a car seat in the driveway because of an epic refried-bean blowout. We still follow each other on social media.

Your Partner

I'm sometimes surprised at the preconceived notions parents seem to have about potty training in general.

"I'LL NEVER GIVE MY KID REWARDS FOR PEEING!"

Or...

"I'LL NEVER LET MY CHILD RUN AROUND NAKED AT HOME WHILE POTTY TRAINING ..."

Or...

"I'LL NEVER DRIVE AROUND WITH A TOILET IN THE BACK OF MY CAR..."

Okay, come back to me in a year and let me know how that worked out. The truth is that the only thing that truly matters is being in agreement with your partner or other key caregivers.

GETTING ON THE SAME PAGE AS YOUR PARTNER

When we set out to potty train our second child, a boy, we knew that we had made some mistakes with our daughter, including not agreeing about the basics, like what we called pee and poop and the words we used to identify the body parts where they came from.

Did we want to use "age-appropriate" terms or go the physiological route? Weiner or penis? Tinkle or urine?

After writing dick and fart jokes for almost 15 years in comedy, I had to reprogram myself to refrain from saying things to my daughter like "Do you need to take a dump?" while my wife said things like "Do you need to go potty?" We were also moving from potty training our daughter to our son, so body parts—and how going potty works biologically—were different.

Making sure we had a conversation about terminology made the second time around easier. When everyone uses the same vocabulary, it prevents your kid from getting more confused during an already confusing process.

Friends and Family

It's important that the people who are a frequent presence in your child's life are also keyed into your plan and implementation process. My mother-in-law has always been a really active part of our kids' lives and has some very good ideas since she's raised four kids and has 11 grandchildren. But one thing we disagreed on is the use of candy or sweets as a reward during potty training. We didn't want our almost-three-year-old to pee little bits nonstop in order to receive chocolate candies as a reward; a "potty dance," a "cheer," or a sticker, sure.

My advice is to be upfront. Once we all talked it through and got on the same page it worked out fine. Plus, I got to eat all the leftover candies.

Potty-Training Professionals

I may have had years of experience in the potty-training process, but I'm not an expert with a degree on the wall. In my humble opinion, seeking advice from people who have been waist-deep in the trenches is some of the best education that exists.

There are a lot of social media support groups, particularly on Facebook, that you can access. There you'll find tons of potty-training successes and failures, but if you really feel as if you're up against the wall and needing more help, you can seek out assistance from actual pros. Most states have certified potty-training professionals who can set up customized plans for you, based on your specific situation and needs. The American Academy of Pediatrics has some helpful guidelines to follow, and your pediatrician may also be able to recommend a local expert.

Be Consistent

Having the ability to be at home during the training process is a crucial part of consistency. To begin, find a time on your calendar with minimal commitments. Take advantage of a long holiday weekend or even possibly consider being homebound for a week or two. Being consistent is key: stick to your decision to start potty training as much as possible, have routines, use similar phrases in your family about the process, and dole out rewards/praise. These strategies will help your little one learn what to expect.

HOW TO NAVIGATE DISRUPTIVE FAMILY CHANGES

Some of the greatest successes in the history of parenting (and beyond) were because people were able to identify starting and finishing lines, but also allow flexibility of thought and process in between.

Our four kids (aged 11, 9, 7, and 2) have lived in seven houses and four states since we started our family, so we know a little something about how life changes and major transitions can cause a legitimate disruption in your life and in that of your potty-training toddler.

Toddlers understand so much more than they can communicate, so if you talk to your little one through coming changes, even if they lack the ability to thoughtfully respond, they will likely understand better. Despite changes in the environment and the ambiance of a bathroom (i.e., in a new home or that of a new caregiver) it's important to emphasize the things that don't change, like a child's potty or where toilet paper is kept.

Communicate Clearly

Communicating with a toddler has its challenges on a good day, but when you throw in a life-altering developmental milestone, it's amped up beyond reason. Try to remember to KISS: Keep It Simple, Stupid. But remember that communication isn't always verbal; it can also be physical, like hand signals. Remember that you do things in a certain order when YOU go to the bathroom, so allow THEM the space to make it a comfortable experience. Listen to their verbal cues, but also be on the lookout for body language that shows signs of happiness or distress.

Take a Break Before You Get Upset

Not only is communication key, but the tone in which you communicate matters. Be mindful of your own frustration levels; you don't want to create negative associations with going to the bathroom; it's already its own vulnerable space. Nobody wants to feel like they're disarming a bomb when they're dropping one. If you feel like you're getting amped up, stop, take a break, and breathe. But fair warning: No matter what you do, don't ever leave a potty-training toddler alone.

It's Totally Normal to Be Frustrated

I am the king of frustrated sounds, comments, quips, huffs, eye rolls, shoulder shrugs, and general passive-aggressive nonsense. I wear my frustration in everyday life like a badge of honor (or a chip) on my shoulder. It is easy to get frustrated during the process of potty training, and honestly, it's expected as well. But try to learn from my mistakes and internalize those moments, or share them later on with your partner or family member. Toddlers are hyper-observant and it's easy to overlook these nonverbal tells that convey how irritated we are, so be mindful and keep them in check.

COMMUNICATION TIPS

Just as communication with your child is important, communicating with your partner or other regular caregivers is just as paramount. When I was at home as the primary caregiver, I was teaching our first child one way of balancing on the toilet seat (hands down at side using the edge of the toilet seat) while my wife on the weekends and at night was encouraging her to place her hands on her knees. Once we talked it through, we realized that, hygienically, her way was better (I'm not totally shocked) and we immediately made training easier for our daughter.

Empathize with Your Child (Learning is Hard Work!)

I'm left-handed, but my wife bought me a right-handed guitar because the guy at the big guitar store told her it would be better to learn on a right-handed guitar. This guitar, although really nice, sat in my office for several years gathering dust until she bought me a left-handed one for a recent birthday.

When I had the guitar that was right for me, I was finally ready to learn . . . but take it from me, learning anything new at any age is hard work, so try and remember to empathize with your child. Get them the right equipment, and (as much as I appreciate my wife trying to surprise me) maybe even include them in the decision-making process. Make it a fun outing to the store for them to pick out underwear they are excited to wear—because they may not be the ones you'd prefer.

Using the potty may seem second nature to us at this point, but try to walk (or crawl) in your child's shoes. The apprehension and fears that they may have while attempting this process can cause a fair amount of stress, which can lead to excessive accidents or possibly even constipation for fear of pooping. You need to make an effort to get down on their level; sit down on the floor of the bathroom and try and establish a dialogue about what might be upsetting them in the moment and how you can make it better.

INSIDE YOUR CHILD'S MIND

For a little one who has defecated in nothing other than a diaper since birth, suddenly sitting over an open hole and pooping is scary. Toilets with loud flushing mechanisms are scary. Sitting high up on the toilet, not knowing if they're going to fall into the water, is scary. Not knowing where that big hole goes to that you're perched on is scary. Making themselves vulnerable (pulling down pants, etc.) and going to the bathroom in a place other than the one they've been accustomed to (their diaper) is scary. Everything about potty training has the potential to be scary for a little one.

Understanding this before ever placing your child on an adult toilet is important—this is why so many parents choose to use potty-training seats that sit on top of a regular toilet, or a child's potty that sits on the ground. There are many types of toilet-training equipment (see Stand-alone Potty, Clip-On Toilet Seat, Padded Themed Seat Overlay on page 55) that will help make the process more enjoyable and less terrifying for your toddler.

Don't Put Pressure on Yourself (Or Your Child)

The worst thing you can do when starting this process is to set up an unrealistic timeline. Flying to Canada in two weeks? Taking a road trip in 16 days? Don't create imaginary deadlines, especially shorter deadlines; don't put undue or unnecessary pressure on yourself because it will transfer to your child.

The last thing you want to do during this training process is give your kid anxiety or traumatize them to the point at which they become fearful of the potty, as that can cause the process to take far longer. If you sense that this is happening, stop. Kids who are scared of the potty tend to hold their waste, and this can cause constipation and kidney damage, and even urinary tract infections if they hold it long enough. If your child is scared, you're likely going to experience more off-potty accidents.

Focus on Progress, Not Perfection

We have one child who refused to go #2 on the potty . . . just refused. I don't know why, but it seemed to scare him. In the beginning, he wouldn't even pass gas without a diaper (which I suppose I should thank him for). He would hold it until we put a diaper back on him. One time he farted while he was sitting down to pee. I laughed (because I laugh anytime I hear a fart) and that moment worked. Every single time he farted, we giggled and cheered. Slow and steady . . .

Enjoy the Process as Much as You Can

As with anything in parenting, it's exhausting tackling each new milestone. But truly, every experience is opening up a world of connective tissue for your toddler as they learn to navigate the world as an independent little being. Watching them change is something that's always been amazing for me and when I can force myself to stop and live in the moment, it makes everything better.

This Can Be Fun!

For our first kid, we bought a Fisher-Price musical potty. We have moved this thing between four states and six houses; we loved it that much. It has its own little toilet paper roll and a working flusher . . . but the best part is that anytime a bodily fluid is released into the toilet bowl, it sings.

There are also a lot of people who are fans of the "potty dance"; search it out on YouTube and you'll never be the same.

DITCH THOSE DIAPERS!

Diapers are expensive, they're unsanitary, and they're (mostly) destroying our planet. Yes, it was kinda cool for a minute to collect points from the diaper boxes and get a few free things, but getting your child out of diapers cannot only save you a ton of money (on average about $50 per month), but it can also keep diapers and wipes from ending up in our landfills. If you're a saver (not me, I'm not a saver), you could put that money into a college savings account for your child.

Once you achieve diaper freedom, consider keeping a few of each size at the house for emergencies when friends are over; you never know when their child might have an accident. You might also consider giving extras to neighbors or friends, or donating them to the local diaper bank.

CHEAT SHEET

If there's anything to glean from this chapter:

1. GET YOUR HEAD ON STRAIGHT. If your child is showing signs or signals that they're ready to potty train, you need to mentally commit to seeing the process through.

2. DISCUSS A PLAN WITH YOUR PARTNER. Once you're in agreement, don't be afraid to share your plan with any immediate or extended family that may be helping you on occasion.

3. MAKE THE TIME. Find a string of days when you can devote a bulk of your time to the process—reminding your child, helping them, etc.

4. TRUST THE PROCESS. There are going to be bumps in the road; stay patient and keep an encouraging tone.

5. CELEBRATE THE SMALL WINS. Any increment of progress is something to be happy about. It's something you can build on.

Conclusion

Getting in the right mindset is the first step toward committing to potty training your toddler. Getting on the same page as your partner, family, and friends is equally important, along with mapping out a strategy. Consistency and communication are crucial, as is managing your frustration and working on patience.

The next chapter covers the ABCs of potty training, from equipment to the actual process. It's about rolling up your sleeves and getting your game on.

PART II

THE ABCS OF POTTY TRAINING

The next two chapters will focus on long lead preparation. We'll discuss all the things that need to be considered BEFORE you even really make it into the physical bathroom: things like the approach when it comes to different sexes, the dialogue and routines that you want to implement, as well as equipment. Potty training happens everywhere; there *will* be accidents. Adding training pants, pull-up-style diapers, or plastic fitted sheets to the shopping list will save a lot of hassle.

CHAPTER 3

Let's Prepare for Potty Training

Potty training isn't just setting your kid on a toilet and hoping for the best; it requires a decent amount of forethought. Avoid choosing a method that operates under the principle of "get it done quick." Although this can seem appealing, it generally means using punishment instead of positive reinforcement, and can create a negative association with the toilet for your child. It also generally means you're training YOURSELF to look for every grimace, every expression, instead of following your child's lead, or putting them on the toilet at specific intervals.

This chapter will focus on how to speak to your child about potty training and what you need to get started.

Introduce the Toilet

Before we get to the actual toilet, first consider what bathroom you're going to use for your toddler's potty-training area. If you live in a small apartment, you probably won't have much to decide on, but if home is a three-story townhouse, you're not going to want to go up and down three flights of stairs every time they have to tinkle.

The chosen bathroom should be in the area where you and your child spend the most time during the day, most likely near the common living space (i.e., kitchen or living room). It should be accessible not only to you, but also to them. With any hope and luck, they'll be able to get themselves to the potty, remove pants, and get seated in a reasonable amount of time (which will become extremely helpful when you're in the middle of deboning a chicken for dinner and they yell "POTTY"). Our daughter Evelyn is at that point right now; she can run and get herself set up, but still needs help with the mechanics of wiping.

Once you've identified where you're setting up shop (this is not as much fun as the amateur woodworking shop I just set up in my garage, but I digress . . .) you have to decide what type of toilet you're going to use: adult toilet, clip-on insert, seat on the toilet, or a stand-alone potty training toilet (see page 55).

Regardless of which you choose, remind your child that, although the water in their tub and the water table outside might be fun to play in, the water in the toilet bowl is in a different category entirely. We try to never touch that bowl aside from peeing and pooping. (We always tussled with the idea of whether we should tell our kids toilet bowls are not a receptacle for matchbox cars, small army men, Barbie clothes, or socks, or if that would just give them ideas. We successfully avoided any major plumbing invoices by not allowing any small toys capable of fitting in that hole in the bathroom area. For distractions, go for allowing the fire truck or hardcover book instead.)

Bring Your Child into the Bathroom with You

As we've discussed, one of the key components to knowing your child is developmentally ready to potty train is by having shown their own keen interest in all that happens in the bathroom.

This could range from anything between:

▶ Asking questions about the potty (i.e., where does the water or waste go?)
▶ Pointing at the potty or wanting to try the flusher
▶ Watching you go and imitating the act by trying to take their diaper off themselves

If they're ready OR you want to create an environment in which their curiosities are acknowledged, they need to be OBSERVING.

From the time we brought our first child home from the hospital, I doubt my wife has ever peed alone. Our kids have literally grown up as an audience to how "big kids" go to the bathroom. Watching their parents is the first step in children understanding how it's done. If you've never peed with a pint-sized observer, now's the time to tackle your stage fright.

Show Them How to Use the Potty

Creating a routine that emulates what adults do every day is important and we'll get to that in the next chapter. For now, let them see you enter the bathroom, put the seat down, pull down or remove your pants, sit down, use toilet paper, flush, and get dressed again. There's a mental conditioning happening, and eventually, they'll be able to mimic the exact process. Incorporating and emphasizing proper hygiene after using the bathroom is also important. Wash your hands, people!

One of the significant things I've noticed my wife doing with our fourth child is reminding her to put her "hands on her knees" while she pees. Remembering that you do not touch the toilet seat is very important.

Explain What Happens

As you go to the toilet, pretend you're the blind leading the blind. Each step that may seem obvious to you is brand new to your child. So say out loud what it is you're doing at each step. This reinforces what your child is seeing you do and will help them remember.

COMMUNICATION TIPS

If your child ever gets truly upset or inconsolable around the idea of using the potty, it's best to completely remove them from the bathroom and allow them to decompress and reset elsewhere. You never want to give your child a negative connotation with the bathroom. Make it a fun place where they're rewarded, not punished.

Aside from the usual practices that help you communicate with your little one, like getting down on their level and making eye contact, it's also important to create a dialogue.

If there was an upsetting moment, take some time to talk about why. I never thought that kids were too young to listen to a simplified explanation of why Daddy got upset and let them know that it was a mistake to get upset—everyone makes mistakes sometimes.

Once you return to the bathroom, it helps to ask the question that relates to the action. For instance, "What do we do first? Do we make sure the toilet seat is down? Yes! Good job!" That kind of reinforcement and positive encouragement can go a long way toward speeding up the education process.

Decide What Language to Use with Your Child (Urine, Pee, BM, etc.)

As we discussed in the previous chapters, staying consistent with the verbiage you and your family use is important.

When deciding what actual terms to use, try and keep in mind that these words will likely make an appearance in your child's vocabulary for a long time, through preschool and into elementary school. Words and phrases that I may not necessarily find offensive—like "crap," "take a dump," or "take a leak"—I'm finding that these seem to ruffle the feathers of some well-intentioned preschool teachers and accompanying administration. So choose wisely.

It's Super Important to Use Terms Consistently

Reinforcing the routine mechanics of going to the bathroom is critical; it's equally important to use repetition in the potty terms that you, your partner, and family have agreed upon.

Having visitors who say things like "make a dooty" or "hose it off" may be funny, but rather inappropriate for your kid's long-term vocabulary. Such terms may even potentially set your child back on their learning process because they may not understand what these people mean. If you have visitors staying for a while, make sure to let them know what terms your family uses.

Stay Positive; Your Child Will Probably Be Nervous

Try not to turn this process into a battle; both your sanity and your relationship with your toddler will thank you. Your tone and body language convey your feelings in these situations. If your toddler seems intimidated or senses that you're getting frustrated with their slow progress, it could have a detrimental psychological effect and create more serious problems down the line. Patience continues to be the key here; if you need to take your own time-out, it's better than creating a negative learning experience.

INSIDE YOUR CHILD'S MIND

This whole process can be very intimidating to a young mind. If, out of nowhere, someone was teaching you to fly an $80 million F-35 fighter jet and your day job is being a cashier at the local market, my guess is that you would feel a bit apprehensive and nervous about sitting in the cockpit.

If we scale it down, your child only knows how to be a kid and, up until now, the diaper has done all the work. Not only can the process of using the toilet be scary, but think about the actual hardware. Some flushes can be very loud and forceful for kids; heck, I've even been startled by some powerful flushes from time to time. And a child sitting on that same potty will likely think they're going to go where the water goes. So have a conversation (or several) with your child to explain how the toilet works and tame that toilet monster.

What to Think About If You Are Potty Training a Child of the Opposite Sex

I'm sure that there are some folks out there who didn't potty train this way, but for many parents it's been easiest and most effective to start children off the same way: sitting down, regardless of sex. All kids will need to eventually poop train, which can often happen at the same time they're sitting down to urinate.

For boys, there are some cool training urinals that attach to the wall or suction to the toilet that can be great for "shooting practice" after your child has the basics down. We did have one of these for our boys, but we tossed it eventually because once they were old enough to actually pee standing up, we just taught them to do it in the toilet.

Why Is Poop Scary to a Child?

I'll just stick my neck out here and say that poop isn't just scary to a child, it's scary to everyone, let's be honest. It comes in various forms. No one likes it. It smells and it's sort of sticky and gross. You're not going to have a romantic relationship with feces during all of this.

Let's hope for your sake, your child carries on this disdain for feces. I'm sure we've all seen the horror pictures of toddlers left unattended that mistook excrement for finger or wall paint.

That said, aside from the obvious nightmare-fuel that poop is, there are also some real physical reasons why your child might be scared to poop—namely discomfort. Constipation is one of the biggest reasons that toddlers are scared to poop, because it can hurt to come out. And a toddler who is having anxiety about the potty will hold it more often, making things worse.

Constipation is common. About one out of every three children suffers from it at some point. Two of the biggest reasons that constipation is so widespread in the toddler age group is due to holding it for too long, or simply forgetting to go because they're busy building forts and generally messing up the house. If your toddler is having fewer than three bowel movements per week, they have constipation.

If you or your pediatrician thinks that your child is experiencing constipation, you can try some of the following remedies:

- **4 OUNCES DAILY OF JUICE.** Sorbitol, a sweetener found in prune, white grape, or pear juice, makes poop more fluid-filled and easier to pass.
- **MASSAGE.** Massaging the abdomen in circular motions or going back to the infant "bicycling the legs" days might help your toddler, but so can, erm, gently massaging your child's anus. In all truthfulness, I've always made my wife do this one, but you can very gently insert the very tip of a cotton swab coated in Vaseline into your child's hiney and that may stimulate your child's poop reflex. I leave this one to my better half. I take care of vomit; she takes care of butts. That's our deal.

- ▶ INCREASE FIBER. Fiber-rich foods include apples, and pears (skin on!), high-fiber cereals, whole-grain breads, berries with seeds, and any and all beans. The bromelain in pineapple acts as a digestive aid, and yogurt commonly contains probiotics that can also help with constipation.
- ▶ INCREASE WATER INTAKE. This one seems simple, but in reality, most of us don't get enough water in a day. Encourage your child to take sips every hour with you if you think they are constipated.

What to Have on Hand

Skilled workers don't show up to the jobsite on Monday morning without the tools they need to get their job done. You don't want to be caught with your pants down (sorry) when it comes time for bathroom education.

Stand-Alone Potty, Clip-On Toilet Seat, Padded, Themed Seat Overlay

These are absolutely must-haves, if you ask me. The adult throne is so large that you need something toddler-sized to fit their little behinds, and with that often comes toddler-themed prints and designs.

Stand-alone potties have a lot of parts to clean, which is definitely a point against them, but these days some include engaging devices that start singing when urine hits the bowl, or that cheer when your child is done. Emphasizing and reinforcing the cause-and-effect process can prevent kids from using these accessories as toys. Let them know that we can't hit the flusher until we go pee or poop; otherwise, we won't get to hear the song. These toilets are also handy if you (eventually) want your child to be able to walk in and pee alone, which our fourth child does—she calls for us when she's ready to wipe.

If you don't have the space for one of these stand-alone units, manufacturers make tons of different child potty seats that you place on top of the adult toilet, and they are generally softer and have handles for little hands. Another type we have used clips onto the toilet seat lid and stays in place with a magnet. When a child has to go, they easily flip it down. It is honestly one of the best solutions for cramped bathrooms or small spaces.

Stool (No Pun Intended) for Toilet and Sink

You may have been gifted one of these at a baby shower, but a step stool is a necessary evil. I say evil because I'm always kicking them out of the way when I use the bathroom. Not only will you likely need to have one for your child if you use a seat that goes on top of the adult toilet, but you will also need one at the sink so your toddler can wash their hands.

Toilet Paper or Flushable Wipes

If you've never had to wipe a writhing toddler after a fresh drop, you're one of the lucky ones. It's one thing to try and wipe them when they're lying down for a diaper change, but toilet paper is not always your friend when you have a toddler bending over asking you to clean their hiney. Flushable/biodegradable wipes are KEY here for a number-two assist. Please be aware that so-called flushable wipes have been banned by many municipalities because they can block up a sewage system. To be on the safe side, do not flush them. Dispose of them the way you would a disposable diaper.

Hardcover Books or Big Toys

We had totally sold out by the time we had baby number four. This little one has a tablet that she uses when she thinks she has to poop. She loves to eat protein bars on the toilet—don't follow our lead here. Just find your kid a great story they love to read. A little bin of bathtub books or hardcover books works great to keep them occupied.

Plastic Bag
(For Emergency Containment)

Always keep a box of gallon storage bags handy. I keep a bag in my backpack, one or two in each car, and while on the road I've even used a dog-poop bag that was connected to an old leash. These are great for isolating wet or soiled clothes after an accident.

At home, we have an over-the-door system of cloth storage bins (over-the-door shoe holders work well, too) that keeps all of our supplies neat and within arm's reach.

Sticker Chart

If you decide your potty-training plan will utilize a sticker chart, you need to pick a spot for it. We always tended to keep it in the kitchen where there was heavy foot traffic to increase bragging rights. A thought on sticker/reward charts: Sometimes, instead of having them be based on actual elimination, you might offer one whenever your child tries, giving them more opportunities to sit on the toilet.

CHEAT SHEET

This was a heavy chapter, but you're already in the mindset to make this happen. All of these details should give you the resources to turn potty training into a reality.

1. **ESTABLISH YOUR HOME BASE.** You don't want to use a bathroom that's out of reach for potty training. Agree on one that's close to a common area.

2. **GEAR UP.** You can't just drop a child on an adult toilet and expect potty training to happen. Look at stand-alone potties, stools for resting feet and reaching the sink, and a few other accessories that might make life easier.

3. **STAY POSITIVE.** Accidents are going to happen a lot; keep your cool, count to 10, and try to offer positive encouragement to your children no matter what happens.

CONTINUED >>>

4. **STAY CHILL.** Ask Alexa to turn on "Patience" by Guns and Roses if you need a reprieve—or say the Serenity Prayer a handful of times—your partner and little one will appreciate your ability to stay calm.

5. **POOP IS SCARY.** It's basic nightmare fuel for all of us, but it can also lead to constipation in a child. Maintain a healthy diet and fluid intake to avoid dealing with it more than you need to.

Conclusion

So, we've covered the ideas behind getting you and your toddler prepared for battle. You've learned what it's going to take to get this expedition from the bottom of the mountain to the top. Persistence and consistency are major factors.

We've talked about considering a vocabulary, routine, and discussed a little bit about the potential equipment and supplies that you'll want to acquire as you get ready to attempt potty training. If you're able to concur with your partner, as well as immediate and extended family that might be involved, that's half the battle.

Now it's time to actually focus on the mechanics.

CHAPTER 4

It's Potty Time

To paraphrase *Saturday Night Live* icons Wayne and Garth: "Potty Time! Excellent!"

You're stocked up—on information and hopefully the equipment and accessories to make this a successful run. Always remember that practice makes perfect—there's no harm in taking baby steps. Get your little one on board by telling them, "You're starting potty training today!" and this is a BIG deal for everyone. Pour on the positivity and compliments and keep your head on a swivel!

Pick a Block of Time for Going Diaper-Free

The best way to get started, in my experience, is to pick a time when you'll be home for several days at a stretch. Perhaps it's spring break for your other kids, a planned staycation, and hopefully not another pandemic.

This idea may be somewhat controversial, but in our house we are big fans of the "let it all hang out" approach to potty training. Lock the doors, drop the blinds (so passersby don't think you've lost all control and call CPS) and everyone, or at least the active potty-training participant, drops the diaper. But with this method, it's not just the diaper, it's the pants, too.

The idea behind this is that kids generally do not like the feeling of pee running down their legs. Having this happen once or twice with a friendly course-correction from the parents will encourage them to find you or the potty before it happens again.

Many parents will take diapers off and keep leggings or pants on. We didn't do this. Without a hiney-cover on, a child's instinct for when they need to go becomes amplified. With this method, expect to be home for several days entirely, and venture outside only as far as your backyard.

If I'm being totally honest, with each of our kids we didn't leave the house for the better part of a week.

You've already heard our story about Ava having an accident in the deli department, but such accidents will begin to happen further and further apart, ultimately happening rarely or never again. Our stay-at-home method has been proven successful many times over and hopefully can create a solid baseline for your child understanding the signals and urges to use the bathroom.

As you begin to assess what will work best for you and your family, you also might want to look into some of the following methods: three-day potty training, parent-led potty training, child-oriented potty training, and, a less popular method in Western culture, infant potty training.

Different potty-training methods and techniques have different timelines. There are some that have you working toward your goal cautiously over a month or more, sans diaper/with pants on, constantly suggesting that it's time to go to the potty.

And there are other methods that boast the ability to get your child mostly potty trained in three to five very messy days. Ultimately, it's up to you to decide which approach will best fit your child and family situation.

Have Your Child Help
You Toss Their Diaper

You can mark the beginning of potty training by having your child walk their diaper out to the big trash can or do something that's different from just tossing it into the Diaper Genie. Make it feel like a big event to them. Allow them to walk YOU through that process.

While ballsy, if you're certain that you are starting this anti-diaper journey and not looking back, give away most of your diapers. Let your child see you give them away so they know that there isn't a fallback. Nevertheless, my better instincts tell you to keep some hidden, just in case.

There will be times throughout this training journey when you may find yourself in need of a diaper or pull-up. For example, a few months after our youngest, Evelyn, potty trained completely during the day, she was still needing a diaper at night or during her longer nap times. As a family, we decided to embark on a road trip. She fell asleep in the car and I needed a diaper to make sure she didn't soil her car seat. While being careful not to send mixed messages, I'm glad I put her in one as a backup, because she went #1 while she was sleeping.

Provide Verbal Reassurance

Kids do well with lots of praise; they work well in a positive environment full of affirmation. It's also a great idea to encourage siblings and/or other members of your family or friends to show their excitement when a job is well done.

I have often been worried about over-rewarding my kids during this process as a means for them to manipulate me into getting what they want. But the reality is that if they're trying, they're trying, and they should be rewarded for that.

COMMUNICATION TIPS

As we've talked about, not all communication is verbal.

When my wife was breastfeeding our infants, she used to reach up and grab her breasts sporadically. I remember thinking to myself, *Having kids is awesome; these are perks no one talks about!* I was a bit deflated when I found out that she was actually just randomly checking to see how full her breasts were or to see if she was leaking. That was a letdown (pun intended).

Using a similar method of checking in can be very helpful for your toddler. Do random underpants inspections throughout the day to make sure they're both dry and "skid-mark-free." It can help you catch an accident quickly. The last thing you want is for your child to become accustomed to wet pants. Plus, such checks will reinforce the idea that dry equates to good.

Practice Undressing Near the Potty

This might seem obvious, but even if you choose to potty train children who are half-clothed or fully naked, there will come a time when your toddler needs to learn to pull their pants up and down, and it's harder for them than you might think. Our fourth child was potty trained for a year before she truly grasped how to pull her undies up over her rear.

During that first week of hardcore potty training, it might make sense to do some practice drills near the toilet and have your child work on getting dressed and undressed as if they had an actual emergency.

HOW TO HANDLE CLOTHING WHEN YOUR CHILD IS POTTY TRAINING

Deciding what method of potty training you're going to use is the first big decision. Are you going to make them stay fully clothed? Are you going to allow them to roam pantsless around the house, or are you going to do what we did (turn up the heat) and allow them carte blanche nakedness? There are plenty of pros and cons for all of these options, but knowing what you, your partner, and your child want is important. For the method we've used, pros include the lack of pants during an accident. The ensuing mess will possibly encourage your toddler NOT to do that again. A potential con is that they may be naked and sitting or playing in areas of the house that may not be clean.

If you choose the fully dressed method, perhaps there's a stool, hamper-top, or basket behind the toilet on which to set their pants and underwear as part of a routine. Unless, of course, it's a last-minute rush and in that event, the routine goes out the window.

For those who are half-dressed or fully naked, it might make sense to keep a pair of underwear and pants where your child is supposed to use the toilet. You can always bring this up matter-of-factly while they go potty, illustrating that this is the destination for those articles in the future.

Slowly Start to Increase Their Liquids

In addition to the milk or other liquids you give your child, they should also be consuming between two and four cups of water per day. An increase in liquids will yield several important results during this losing-the-diapers phase: it will hydrate them even further, it will cause them to need to urinate more frequently, and it will decrease the chances of constipation.

If your child hasn't had water as a drinking option up until this point, it could be a great time to buy them a special water cup—sippy cups, cups with fun or silly straws, spill-proof, topple-proof, or anything in between. Sometimes kids who are used to milk or juice are water-averse. If we are being utterly honest here, one of the best ways to sneak water into their diet is by slowly starting to cut their normal expected liquids like milk or juice with ⅓ water. Then after a couple days, add in more. If they seem to be onto you with the ⅓ water, cut it back a bit. You can also give your kids saltier snacks, or snacks that might make them want a drink of water, such as apples dipped in salted nut butters. Anything you can do to increase their desire for liquids helps, because it increases trips to the potty, which increases your chances of success.

Learn to Read Your Child's Signs

Throughout your journey as a dad, you've likely come into contact with a whole slew of people quick to provide opinions and external pressure on how and when to potty train. Many of these people—grandparents, preschool administrators, and other parents—are incredibly well-intentioned and may be full of knowledge and real-life wisdom, but you and your partner are the ones who truly KNOW your child. Here's what to look for as signs you should rush your kid to the bathroom:

Going from Rambunctious to Quiet

If your typically loud and even wild toddler starts to get quiet, you can tell that something is going on. This is a big sign for anything physical, emotional, or even mental, and always cause for the dad-gut to go "wait a minute . . . " Anytime a little one gets quiet, you know shit is quite literally about to hit the fan.

Escaping to Sit or Be Alone in a Corner

Kids don't necessarily like to poop with an audience; I mean, would you? I triple-lock the bathroom door when I get time alone on the throne. When we were potty training our third child, when it came time to push, he would hold up his hand and say, "Don't look," and we happily went back to playing on our phones. If you notice your child making an escape to a corner or less-trafficked part of the house to go to the bathroom, it could be a general fear of the toilet—many children are afraid of the idea of pooping on the toilet. If that's the case, take time to introduce and acclimatize your child to the toilet again.

Squatting or Looking Pensive for Extended Periods of Time

Ever heard of the Squatty Potty? It's an as-seen-on-TV product that lets you bring your feet up closer to the toilet, thereby allowing you to bear down and giving you ample pushing ability. Apparently squatting is the best form of pooping (who knew?), and if you notice your toddler taking to the ground as if they're going for the world record in squats, you might need to step in, stat.

Picking and Tugging at Their Pants

This could be a sign that your child is about to go, trying too hard to "hold it," or even trying to physically, with their hand, keep the pee or poop from coming out. Other times it can be a signal that there may be something bothering them, a painful feeling or a pressure that's unnatural to them, in which case ask them what they're feeling in their body.

Use Verbal Prompts

I sometimes wish that there was a consistent, uniform prompt to get kids to go to the bathroom.

Some of the classics include:

▸ *"Do you need to go pee-pee?"*

- *"Do you need to go potty?"*
- *"Is it potty time?"*
- *"Is the pee-pee ready to come out?"*
- *"Do you want to sit on the toilet?"*
- *"Do you want to go to the bathroom now?"*

Try to learn from my mistakes with our first child and refrain from the ol' "Do you need to take a crap?" Make sure that all caregivers in your child's life, from preschool teachers and step-parents to babysitters and grandparents, know what words you've chosen to use.

I think it can sometimes be difficult to ask toddlers questions because they understand the *tone* of a question and possibly even their expected response, but they may not actually understand the content. They might throw a quick "no" at you because they think that's what you're expecting to hear. So, if you're asking questions and hearing "no" as a response, but keep seeing accidents, you might want to make the switch from questions to statements, such as:

"Make sure to tell us when you need to use the potty!"

"I've set the potty up for you so you can go whenever you get that funny feeling."

"Remember to stop and go to the potty soon."

When They Are Ready, Place the Child on the Toilet

If they aren't kicking and screaming at this point, then you're probably ready to give it a shot.

UNDRESS: First, allow them to step out of their underwear and pants (if you're potty training with clothing) in front of the toilet.

HOP ON: Next, sit them down on the toilet. If there's an initial fear about sitting on the toilet, having a kid-themed potty chair can help, but you could also demonstrate the process yourself. Watching you sit down on the toilet and witnessing a normal experience could calm their nerves. If they absolutely refuse, it could be time to back off, reset, and give it a try later in the day, week, or month.

LET GO: Now tell them to "let the pee-pee out." It's important, in my opinion, to get them thinking early on that they control the flow of the urine. Equating the release of urine to using a hose outside to water the plants or making similar references might help the process along. Reassure them that the toilet is an appropriate place to do what they already did in their diaper.

CHANGE THE TOPIC: Keep the bathroom stocked with books to read or even a tablet for some games or cartoons. The minutes can seem like hours, and reading or watching something can help them relax. Books about going potty starring some of their favorite cartoon characters can also help the situation.

GET CLEAN: There are several different wiping techniques. My recommendation would be to use the way that you were taught—what comes naturally to you will be easier when it comes time for instruction.

FINISH UP: Leaving the bathroom the way you found it (hopefully it was clean to begin with) is also important. Show your child how to check that we didn't make a mess, flushed successfully, and closed the toilet seat and lid. Make sure to include pulling up pants, washing hands, and potentially getting a reward if that's an incentive program that you've adopted.

No one ever warned me about how LONG it takes to pee on the potty—not just the whole process, but also each time you set your little one down on the toilet. Sometimes it's a quick 10 seconds, and other times it's five minutes. On average, it should take between three and five minutes for them to pee. Be careful not to repeatedly have them sit on the toilet for longer, unless of course they want to. Otherwise, it could begin to feel like a punishment.

Potty Training a Child of the Opposite Sex

Potty training doesn't differ too much based on sex, especially if you're starting both of them sitting down. Remember from your recent diapering days that boys are equipped with a firehose that is hard to aim down at times—there are chances that you'll encounter the occasional erection. Pushing the penis down is much better than taking a direct hit while you are helping. Know that girls have to be wiped front to back. Other than that, it's a pretty unisex process.

WHAT ARE SOME COMMON POTTY-TRAINING TRAPS TO AVOID?

▶ Don't begin potty training during stressful times in your life unless it's absolutely unavoidable. Starting preschool or daycare, for example, can be a time when, due to licensing, your child must be diaper-free. But if someone is starting a new job or pregnant with a sibling, try not to add stress to other big life changes.

▶ Don't set short deadlines, especially unrealistic ones. I'm a big fan of the "sometime this year you'll be potty-trained" mentality versus the three-day method.

▶ Don't make a big deal about accidents in pants or on the floor; simply clean them up and allow your child to help. Accidents are how we learn what not to do, and as much as it will be a signal to your child, it will help you learn how to help them as well.

▶ Don't be afraid to stop and wait another few weeks or months to start potty training if it's just not working. Just don't make it a pattern, since stopping and starting repeatedly will send your child mixed messages.

▶ Don't use fancy clothes or lots of layers. When you're starting out with this process, naked is best. If you can't or don't want to do naked, then for everyone's sanity, try to do no pants.

How You Talk to Your Child at This Stage Is Key

As we have discussed in the previous sections, success in potty training is unlikely to happen without tears and accidents along the way—expect them from your child as well. In all seriousness, it's important that you stay calm and try to communicate with your toddler in a way they can understand.

It's paramount to use language that reminds your little one that they are in control of their pee. They get to decide when it comes out, and when it does, it's cause for celebration.

Clearly Explain
What Is Happening at All Times

I always felt like potty training was similar to assembling a piece of furniture from Ikea or following a recipe. If you skip a step, it's not gonna turn out right. Same thing applies here. I almost pretend that someone can't see what we're doing and is only listening to the audio; each step has to be described, performed, and celebrated. Even things that you don't think need to be detailed, such as what's going to happen when the poop falls out, where it goes when it's flushed, and why they won't fall in are worth explaining to your little one.

Choose Encouragement

Creating a negative association with the bathroom could be one of the worst things that can happen in attempting this process, so lead with positive phrases or tones. Ask questions and congratulate them for getting steps right (or even remotely close with correction, if needed). Kids should be excited to not only use the bathroom as a new experience, but also find your encouraging words and sentiments a self-esteem and self-confidence builder.

Don't Criticize

I mastered the art of potty training more than 40 years ago, so yeah, it's pretty easy for me to pick apart a rookie's approach. But they're the student and you're the teacher. Criticizing failed technique or attempts, or even becoming angry during that type of bathroom interaction is detrimental and does nothing to build up your child's sense of self-worth.

INSIDE YOUR CHILD'S MIND

At the very core of every child and every situation involving one is a child who deeply and truly wants to please their parents. You have to keep that in mind every time you escort them to the bathroom or potty. They look up to you as their guardian and protector, someone who will never let them fall (into the potty) and always be there as a beacon of support. That said, this crap is difficult. It's one of those parenting processes in which it is super easy to tell parents to be chill and try to be patient, or to say "someday you'll look back on this and laugh," but the reality is easier said than done. You have the power to make or break your child's spirit, so every time they pee or poop in the potty, even if some gets smeared on the seat, you cheer for them like nobody's business.

Celebrate Every Success

There are numerous YouTube Kids potty songs, dances, and ways to celebrate. Kids at this age take great pride in making Mom or Dad happy. If you chose to create a sticker chart or similar reward program, then use images or stickers that they choose. And perhaps for every grouping of positive potty experiences, they get to trade those in for a new bathroom book for continued entertainment.

CHEAT SHEET

In my opinion, this was our most challenging chapter because we're actually doing it instead of just talking about it.

1. **EXPECT ACCIDENTS.** Be positive and don't make a big deal about accidents. Accidents will be a lot less painful on all of you if you just proactively add "clean up puddle of pee in kitchen" to your to-do list.

2. **AVOID WARDROBE MALFUNCTIONS.** Choose clothing that is easy for a toddler to manipulate. Once you decide it's time to put the pants back on, or if you never take them off, remember that dresses are long and can get caught under your toddler's hiney. Pants with snaps or buttons are more difficult for fingers already dealing with dexterity issues.

3. **LEARN TO READ YOUR CHILD'S PHYSICAL CUES.** If they are squatting, walking away alone, looking pensive, or otherwise changing their behavior, remind them to tell you if they have to go.

CONTINUED >>>

4. **COLLABORATE WITH CARETAKERS.** Make sure all adults in your toddler's life are on the same page about what words to use, as well as the training process as a whole.

5. **CELEBRATE THE SUCCESSES!** Despite how normal or routine you may find any one action when it comes to potty training; celebrate it as a win with your toddler. Knowing that they're getting all the steps right is an important confidence builder!

Conclusion

Hopefully after everything we've talked about thus far, you're feeling confident in the foundation of beginning potty training, including verbal prompts. By now you've got an idea of how to actually potty train—not just the method, but also how to introduce kids to the bathroom and how to get them to use it.

Coming up, we'll be exploring how to navigate the process while you're in the midst of it. We'll talk about successes, tracking progress, and recovering from accidents.

CHAPTER 5

Practice Makes Perfect

Practice makes perfect, but so does process. You feel like you've got your head in the right space. You've got an approach. You've got the equipment, supplies, and time carved out to take this thing head on. But you've got to keep in mind that while it looks good on paper, it may not always grab on the first take.

In this chapter, we'll look at how you're going to need to pivot, evolve, and adapt on the fly to find the best methods and practices that make this work for your child. With trial, error, a little bit of perseverance, and a whole lotta patience, you might just find yourself at the finish line, focusing more on post-potty hygiene than the actual process itself.

You Did It! Now, Let's Do It Again

Dads, pull up a chair, grab your favorite beverage, and prepare yourself for an epic binge-watching (and participating) session because nothing with potty training comes quickly. You'll be repeating the steps in the previous chapter until your child is comfortable with the process.

It's important to note that with all children, bladder control comes before bowel control, and the ability to potty train for short periods of time during waking hours comes long before the ability to manage those abilities through the night.

While potty training, I always took my kids to the bathroom as if it were the first time, reintroducing the process so it became ingrained in their minds. After explaining it many times, I advise shifting to a more interactive experience, asking them rather than telling them.

"What do we do first when we have to use the potty?"

"Once we go pee-pee or poop, what do we do next?"

"When we're finished, how do we flush the toilet?"

"And before we leave the bathroom, how do we wash our hands?"

It felt very reminiscent of the "Choose Your Own Adventure" books that I read in my adolescence. After a few rounds, the idea is that the process becomes a habit, just like any other routine.

Get Comfortable with Trial and Error

There are going to be accidents, even if they don't happen initially, and patience is the key personality trait that you'll need to bring to the table.

Make that run to your local bulk discount store to invest in paper towels and carpet, tile, and hardwood floor cleaner. Also, make sure to control your responses to these accidents. Just like our kids, we parents have inherent and often immediate reactions to something going wrong. If I'm riding in someone's blind spot on the freeway and they cross over and inadvertently cut me off, I may have some choice words and finger actions to let them know. But you're dealing with a much more delicate situation. You don't want to create a negative correlation between potty-training accidents and consequences. Accidents are unavoidable.

Some kids get so into playtime that they either don't want to stop and pee or they don't remember to. This is when you put your foot on the gas by gently reminding them that they may need to go potty, while rewarding them with kind words and tone.

Figure Out What Works Best for You and Your Child

Finding the routine that works for each child might be one of the toughest, yet most integral parts of making this process a success. Not every piece of advice that I've offered in this book will work for your child in the way that it's presented.

My wife and I chose to go the "take a week off, become hermits, and let them run wild and free with no bottoms" route, but perhaps this doesn't work in your household. Maybe it works best with them wearing underwear and no pants. Maybe it works best to set an alarm on your phone every 30 or 60 minutes to remind yourself to ask them if they need to go. This may seem like a major inconvenience, but it will be short-lived. Once you see the reduction in accidents and your child achieves a successful grasp of the process, you'll know that your flexibility paid off.

KEEP TRACK OF YOUR CHILD'S PROGRESS

Every year, my accountant asks me to keep a log of business miles that I've driven and every year I find myself cursing him out and scrambling to sync my gas diary with my calendar. Honestly, it's a pain in the ass. BUT it would get me out of hot water with the IRS if my claims were challenged.

The same theory applies here. Sometimes you're so DEEP in the process that you can't see the forest for the trees. Keeping a log of your progress (positive or negative) is a great barometer for looking back to see where you stand. Being able to look at recorded data will allow you to fine-tune your approach or identify what's working versus what isn't. Keep a journal of your own, or take pics of potty charts if you're using those. If you're using the naked method and start to see a string of successes—when the urge to go is matched with an equal motivation to get to the potty—you could be getting very close to trying out some underwear and eventually pants.

No need to thank my accountant; he already gets paid too much.

Use Rewards and Positive Reinforcement

My wife and I try and live by the idea of positive reinforcement with our kids. There's little success or forward progress with negative thinking and thought. Criticism or embarrassment doesn't seem to work with anything, and it shouldn't be a surprise it won't work with potty training, either.

Rewards and incentives are things that would make our own ears perk up in adult life, and the same concept applies to children. A positive approach can be helpful, but couple this with some form of reward program and you'll double your chances for success.

Intrinsic vs. Extrinsic Rewards

There's been a lot of research in recent years on what motivates humans to do what we do. There are both internal or "intrinsic" motivators (wanting to feel happy, be proud of yourself, etc.) and external or "extrinsic" motivators (winning an award, getting a promotion, etc.).

When it comes to potty training, an intrinsic motivation could be going to the bathroom because it's inherently exciting or makes a child feel like a grown-up. On the other hand, extrinsic motivation would be getting a reward or prize for attempting or completing a task related to potty training.

There's some suggestion that there's a slippery slope with the use of extrinsic rewards: that once a child becomes accustomed to being rewarded for tasks, they may eventually want to know "What will you give me for it?" or "What's in it for me?"

That being said, the use of rewards for potty training worked for us and none of our kids seemed to assume that meant that they would be rewarded for other tasks. And, eventually, they stuck to using the toilet without them.

Different Types of Rewards

There are a few ways to incentivize your children to pay attention to the process of potty training. Some of these have worked with our kids; some haven't. A good way to approach this could simply be to take the one that you're most comfortable doing and ask your child if it makes them excited. I wouldn't recommend throwing these all out there—you might be on the hook for more than one!

STAR CHARTS. Many schools use a similar type of chart to reward students for things such as good behavior and attendance, reading achievements, or success in math. These types of charts tend to do well when displayed in a prominent location like on the fridge or bathroom door.

REWARD APPS. There are a ton of digital reward apps in which you give your kids coins, stars, or icons for a job well done. Perhaps suggest to them that they can turn these in for a prize. But try to keep in mind that prizes should always be realistic for their age group.

FOOD OR CANDIES. This is something that I've mentioned before. Little kids need only a small piece of candy or edible treat each time, in essence one M&M or other small snack. Using this model, you may want to be mindful of their sugar intake, as well as their potentially taking advantage of the opportunity and urinating less each time, but increasing the frequency in order to rob you of all of your chocolates.

DANCE PARTIES. Hop on Amazon, buy yourself one of those karaoke microphones, and go to town with some old school Prince, Beastie Boys, or the Police. Or just crank up the Cocomelon and bust out some dance moves in the kitchen while making dinner after the two of you complete a successful trip to the bathroom.

STICKERS. Pick up a sketchbook or bound journal with blank pages (dollar stores have a plethora of options). And if your child is as gullible as mine, both the grocery store and Target have free stickers at checkout. (Do they still make scratch 'n' sniffs?)

If none of these seem attractive to your child, ask them. Perhaps they have a suggestion that's within reason.

Accidents Happen

Accidents do, in fact, happen. It's something you'll just have to get used to. Truly. Invest in some good ol' cleaner and start waiting. It would be wise to never punish your child for a potty accident, whether it's at home or out in public. Nor should you yell or act irritated at the process. No one is perfect, especially young kids who are learning something completely new. Yelling, scolding, or punishing can damage your child's relationship to the potty, but also, equally important, your relationship with your child. Not only can this kind of negative attention work against you, it can also make your child regress in any progress they've made.

Common Accidents

NAPTIME OR NIGHTTIME BED-WETTING. Daytime proficiency doesn't mean anything after the sun goes down. Bed-wetting is generally considered very normal and developmentally appropriate. We have one child who wet the bed every single night for YEARS. We took him to a nephrologist, a urologist, and a neurologist who all said the same thing . . .

> "Boys typically take longer than girls, and some boys won't be able to stop bed-wetting until they're 12. At 13, we consider there might be an underlying issue."

When you start potty training your son at two and all of a sudden realize that you could have a decade or more of bed wetting, it can be defeating, for you AND for your child. Do what you can to minimize the frustration and potential embarrassment. Pull-ups or plastic fitted sheets under your regular fitted sheet can certainly help.

ROAD TRIPS. Car trips get longer with potty training—or newly potty-trained children. I take no pride in saying that I've probably used 80 percent of the gas stations or Welcome-Center lavatories up and down the Eastern seaboard. I always said there were two things I would never do as a parent: buy a minivan and have a toilet in my truck. So far, I've only caved to one of those. Investing in a telescoping car urinal and/or a foldable car potty seat can be a lifesaver.

TRAINING PANTS. Don't be afraid of the pull-ups for situations in which you aren't sure you'll be able to get to a bathroom quickly or if you are sick and tired of washing your car-seat insert. If you're out on a hike or nature walk, or end up somewhere with limited restroom access, you may want to make sure your child knows they're going to be able to go. This is really only in a dire situation, though, and what you'll likely find is that they won't WANT to pee in their pull-up, even if there is no other option.

PEEING ON THE FLOOR. Anytime you have a potty-training toddler with or without pants on, you risk having urine on everything. Be prepared for pee (or poop) accidents. Never in my life did I think I'd be talking out loud to myself, saying something like "Is that a turd over there in the corner?"

POOPING IN PANTS. Seriously, you wouldn't believe the amount of crap I've scrubbed out of underpants. It isn't a case of "Whoops, I forgot" but more a case of "Guessed wrong" or "I thought it was a fart." Our fourth child still doesn't understand that a fart isn't the same thing as a poop.

Solutions for Accidents

LET YOUR CHILD HELP YOU CLEAN UP. Allow them to see that there are consequences to every action. If they can help you grab a roll of paper towels and watch as you clean, they might begin to understand that they were responsible and thus make a stronger effort to get to the potty or to make you aware when they have to go.

BEDWETTING ALARMS. My wife generally goes to bed before I do, and I tend to take that time to squeeze in all of my mafia, shoot 'em up, and survival shows. Around midnight is when I used to check on the kids and occasionally take those who were potty training and sit them on the toilet. It definitely cut down on the number of sheets we had to wash in the morning.

MAKE A JOKE OUT OF IT. "That pee-pee wants to go to its potty!" I never thought in a million years that we would be assigning personalities and identities to urine, but hey, if it works, don't knock it.

DOGGIE PEE PADS. These came clutch for more than just our canine. We didn't hesitate to drop one on the bed, sofa, or rug if our toddler was going to be sitting and playing for any extended period of time.

NIGHTTIME HELPERS. Padded training underpants or overnight diaper trainers were our go-to for the overnights, as was limiting the amount of fluids that the kids were drinking close to bedtime.

KEEPING A STASH OF DRY CLOTHES

Just as it's a good idea to keep extra diapers in your diaper bag, backpack, or vehicle for emergencies, the same applies to potty training. If you've already gone through the "stay home" method and you're feeling confident enough to get out of the house—it's important to keep a dry backup outfit or pair of pants handy.

I always made sure that I had an extra pair of underwear, shorts or pants, and plenty of disposable wipes stashed in the back of our car or at the bottom of my dad bag.

It doesn't get more inconvenient than having to drape toddler pants over the dashboard in an attempt to dry them with the A/C or heat while your kid sits naked in their car seat. And yes, I'm speaking from personal experience.

Wiping, Handwashing, and Other Important Hygiene Tips

If there's a silver lining to COVID-19, it might be the increased focus on personal hygiene. That said, kids are likely going to need help wiping for the first year or more. They simply do not command the dexterity nor the balance to wipe well.

By default, potty-training toddlers who are being wiped by an adult need to wipe front to back. This is the same way many women wipe so that fecal matter doesn't get near sensitive urinary tract areas (not knowing this remains one of the most embarrassing moments I can remember as a dad). For poops, make sure you have bio-degradable wipes on hand.

Following wiping, handwashing is going to be the most important part of the bathroom hygiene game. Make sure to show your child how to wash, using soap and warm water, rubbing in between each of their fingers and at their nail beds. One helpful hint is to have them sing the "Happy Birthday" song while washing to make sure they've done it long enough.

HOW MANY ACCIDENTS ARE TOO MANY?

Accidents are DEFINITELY going to happen while potty training. In a recent survey by MadeForMums that involved over 1,200 parents, less than a third (28 percent) of parents said they successfully potty trained their child during a first attempt.

On the first day without diapers, nearly a third (31 percent) of children had three or four accidents, with another 12 percent having five to seven accidents. Most of these kids were aged between 18 and 30 months.

You're in the company of many parents who have experienced accidents.

CHEAT SHEET

1. **PRACTICE MAKES PERFECT.** Consistency and routine should prove successful in the end. Even if your child doesn't have to go potty at that moment, you can always practice by asking them to show you where certain things are (i.e., toilet paper, flusher, etc.).

2. **ACCIDENTS WILL HAPPEN.** As long as you know that, with each hour of every day you'll be mentally prepared for the worst, while hoping for the best.

3. **TRY, TRY, AND THEN TRY AGAIN (PERHAPS IN A DIFFERENT WAY).** If the routine that you created isn't working, identify the hiccup or the problem and be flexible about making adjustments.

4. **REWARDS CAN MAKE A DIFFERENCE.** No need to go overboard with this, but stickers are a small motivator that children can see accumulate.

5. **PRACTICE GOOD HYGIENE.** Feels like this goes without saying, but reinforcing good handwashing techniques as part of your routine will likely carry on into adulthood.

Conclusion

Trial and error is part of figuring out what routine and method of potty training will work for your individual child. Finding an incentive and pushing past accidents with persistence and a supportive dialogue will bring you closer to achieving diaper freedom.

You're halfway home, but there are certainly difficult situations ahead: Naptime, nighttime, and regressions are all things that you'll likely have to contend with.

PART III

POTTY TRAINING 2.0

Once you've got the actual process of potty training down, you can't just plan to NEVER leave your house again. You've got to build up confidence within yourself and in your little one—confidence that you, and they, can successfully venture out into the real world with the ability to find and use a restroom.

This next part of the book will talk about every curveball that you could be thrown, as well as how to handle hitting the road for trips and playdates.

CHAPTER 6

Difficult Situations

Potty training during the day is a challenge in its own right, but once you've got a grip on it, you need to think about those times when your child is, well, sleeping. Naptime can be a challenge, but it's a goal you have to shoot for and make before you tackle the ultimate potty-training beast: nighttime.

My hope is that after reading this chapter, you'll feel equipped to be able to take on that beast as well as other difficult situations that seem impossible to navigate at first: medical issues and what to do with those kiddos who don't seem to want to be potty trained at all.

How to Handle Naptime

Just when you think you've got it all down and you're doing victory laps around the kitchen island, you get to the point in the day when your child needs to lie down to take a nap. Will they be able to maintain any form of bladder control while they rest? Children around 18 months will likely have much less control than that of a three-year-old.

Watch Their Fluids

One of the first steps toward a dry naptime is watching a child's fluid intake. Cut out fluids about 30 to 60 minutes before their normal naptime. Have your little one use the potty just before they're ready to rest.

For many reasons, you should not put your child down to sleep with a bottle or sippy cup, and potty training is another reason.

The following numbers are a helpful guide (though every kid's body parts are unique) and will help you plan ahead:

▶ (From birth through 12 months) An infant's bladder holds one or two ounces and takes one hour to fill from the time they drink.

- (Aged one to three years) A toddler's bladder holds three or four ounces and takes about two hours to fill.
- (Ages four to 12) A child's bladder holds seven to 14 ounces and it can take two to four hours to fill.

Have Them Wear Pants

I recommend pull-up-style training pants during a child's nap.

As they get more mature in potty-training prowess, switch to underpants. I know you're probably saying, "I thought you said that naked was best!" Bear with me, readers—in my humble opinion, naked IS best when potty training . . . but not during naptime. We actually tried naked from the waist down with almost all of our kids, and more times than not, during naps, it didn't work. Something about the cool air hitting their midsection made them wet the bed every single time.

Ending Naptime

Once your child wakes up, the first instinct they will likely have is to pee. Make sure to get them out of bed at the first wake/cry, so that they don't go in their pants. As soon as I used to hear my son stir, I would start shouting up the stairs "Hi, Charlie! Hold your pee! Let's go potty!"

Accident(-Free) Zone

You may experience one of three outcomes after naptime.

1. **High and Dry:** You've got instant success with this approach and your child is able to nap with no pee incident whatsoever.

2. **The Dribbler:** A child who tends to dribble a little bit here and there more than likely doesn't have that ability to hold and consolidate yet but should improve over time. Dribbling is a good sign of control, really, considering the size of a toddler's bladder—it means that they started to go, and then they stopped. Congratulate them.

3. **Soggy Sagger:** The third type could unfortunately be a child with a full-blown soaked diaper. This might be indicative of a child who is resisting going to the bathroom and is waiting for the diaper before releasing themselves. From my experience, kids who sit in wet diapers when they are infants tend to be more comfortable in wet diapers as toddlers. My wife and I rarely let our kids sit in soggy diapers because we wanted them to be disgusted by the feeling, thus helping in the future potty-training process. Keep an eye on the frequency of accidents. You don't want children to normalize them. Switch up your strategy to include increasing the amount of time without fluids before naptime.

How to Handle Nighttime

If you thought navigating through naptime dry was a challenge, nighttime is an entirely different ball of wax.

There are, of course, the random kids who potty train instantly overnight and there could be a reason for that:

- They might not sleep as deeply.
- Perhaps they don't drink as much fluid throughout the day and into the evening.
- They might eat foods that contain less water.
- They might have larger bladders.
- They might have a more mature sense of their urination needs.

Unfortunately, it can sometimes take years of trying before your now 10-year-old will actually be trained to get through the night dry.

Prep the Bed

In an effort not to ruin expensive mattresses, there are many fitted mattress protectors for this purpose, as well as waterproof sheets. There are disposable mattress covers as well, but something long-term and washable is a less expensive option. Coupling these items with pull-ups or nighttime underwear will create much less mess.

Watch Their Fluids

Cutting out fluids between 30 to 60 minutes before bed-time can significantly cut down on accidents!

Have Them Wear Pants

There are nighttime training pants on the market specifi-cally designed for children (including older ones) who are working on making it through the night.

Nighttime Pee

With our first child, we started putting her to bed with a pull-up on. Then several hours later, around 11 p.m., I'd get her up for a nighttime pee. She'd be barely awake, couldn't even hold herself upright on the potty, and we'd tell her to "let the pee-pee out." She'd do her thing, then I'd wipe her and tuck her back in bed.

With our second child, as I write this, we are still working on nighttime issues. And just as simple as our first child's process was, this is categorically normal as well. We tried the nighttime pee, but he would then go back to sleep, wake up slightly around 5 a.m., pee in his pull-up, and go back to sleep. A reduction in fluids before bed, coupled with potentially two nighttime pees and an immediate morning visit to the bathroom, has begun to show success.

Morning Routine

It's important for parents to get into the routine of showing their children that using the potty first thing in the morning is a healthy practice. In the morning, if your child is wearing wet nighttime pants, these obviously get removed and tossed right away. If you begin to see a string of dry nighttime pull-ups, you may want to consider making the shift to underwear or simply pajama pants.

FINDING A SUCCESSFUL DIALOGUE

Toddlers have more synapses firing in their brains between birth and three years of age than at any other time in their life. They are sponges; they will learn—but they will also start to adopt your communication style as their own. One of the pivotal pillars of potty training is finding a way to communicate successfully with your little one in a way that inspires them, not demeans them. Stay positive because young children are very good at reading both vocal and physical cues, and the quiet grumbling you're doing while cleaning up their sheets isn't doing anything to help them.

If there happens to be an accident, regression, or setback, keep a positive tone and use words of encouragement to comfort them, as they're probably feeling down about the situation.

Letting them know that these things happen and that it will be alright will help keep them on the right track.

How to Handle Medical Issues

Our second child was still potty training during naps when our third child breezed right past him, due to a medical issue. Our third child was born with what essentially amounts to three kidneys.

We found this out right before delivery and we were admittedly terrified. His third kidney was misdiagnosed as a tumor, and it sent me and my wife into an utter tailspin for days before they confirmed what it was. Partially due to this anomaly, and partially due to the fact that he had an abnormally large bladder—the size of an adult male's—he didn't have the urge to go as often as other kids.

He was fully potty trained at two and has literally never had a real accident. This is obviously a condition over which we had no control, but it inadvertently put us in a good position when it came to potty training. #silverlining

There are other issues that could be considered medical in nature but which complicate potty training much more.

Holding Urine

If children are forced to begin potty training before they are physically and emotionally ready, you might end up with a toddler who holds their urine. Chronic urine-holding is the underlying cause of almost all potty-training problems. All of them. What does this mean, you ask? These include pee and poop accidents, bedwetting during naps, nighttime sleep, infrequent urination, and also UTIs. If you're noticing this behavior, it may just be too early to begin the potty-training process. Consult with your pediatrician to further explore dysfunction your child may be experiencing.

Constipation

Constipation—pooping fewer than three times a week—is an extremely common problem with young kids. Many times it can be resolved by a change in diet. Eating fruits and vegetables high in fiber, as well as making sure the child is drinking enough daily fluids, can often turn it around. Constipation can also be the result of withholding a bowel movement, like holding urine. In some cases, if children are encouraged to potty train too early, the result could be an unwillingness to poop.

Here are some foods the National Institute of Health recommends for relieving constipation (along with plenty of water):

▸ Whole grains, such as bread, pasta, oatmeal, and bran flake cereals

- Legumes such as lentils, black beans, kidney beans, soybeans, and chickpeas
- Fruits such as berries, apples (skin on), oranges, and pears
- Vegetables such as carrots, broccoli, green peas, and collards
- Nuts such as almonds, peanuts, and pecans

Based on the age of your potty trainer, you might want to consult with your pediatrician on what might work best.

Other Medical Concerns

Blood in stools or in urine, or blood in underpants, abdominal swelling, cloudy or foul-smelling urine, etc., are examples of when you need to get on the phone with your doctor, right away.

Psychological Readiness/Behavior

If children are truly stressed and anxious over the potty-training process, it isn't going to end well for anyone. Stop and reset yourself and your child. Give it a couple weeks and then try again. There are three things that work together to help a child potty train.

1. Knowing where your child is developmentally and emotionally (are they interested in the potty; do they have long periods of dry diapers?)
2. Knowing your child's unique personality (are they naturally an anxious child or an easily excitable or outgoing one?)
3. Understanding what they are physically capable of at their age (what they might be able to do at two is vastly different from three)

Stress

If your little one isn't ready to use the toilet, they may have increased anxiety and fears about being pushed into the act. It's really a harsh thing to try to potty train children on an unrealistic timeline or schedule. High levels of stress can cause a negative impact on your child's brain and on their emotional development as a whole. For example, sometimes using an adult-sized toilet will leave kids' feet dangling in the air, which can create an element of fear. Getting a stool for their feet to rest on can help, but a better solution for this sort of child is to get them their own miniature-sized toilet.

POTTY TRAINING MULTIPLES

Although we have never raised multiples, I feel like we got a sneak peek into what that might be like with Charlie and Mason. Mason was two when he potty trained and at the same time Charlie was four and a half and still going through the process. While both were developmentally appropriate, we made sure to never, ever compare them, nor to compare them to other children.

Comparison does nothing positive and can cause an unnecessary problem between siblings. Early on, our third child once said something to the effect of "Yeah, Charlie, your DIAPER" to his older brother, who was still working through some issues. We nipped that in the bud really fast. I imagine it's similar when you have twins or triplets going through the process, because no children will be identical in their path to diaper independence. If you're dealing with twins or two children who are both ready to potty train, it would certainly make sense to train them at the same time. The companionship and competition could be a benefit. And if you have only one toilet, it might make sense to acquire two stand-alone toilets in the event that the urge hits them at the exact same moment.

How to Handle a Child Who Does Not Want to Be Potty Trained

When I sat down to write this book, I honestly had no idea what I was going to tell you in this section, but the bottom line (pun intended) is that this too shall pass—eventually.

Some kids are truly not ready to potty train, even though all of the signs and signals are there. Other kids have sensory issues that can cause them to like the feeling of having a diaper on, or not like the idea that something is leaving their body and falling into an abyss (aka the toilet).

There are a few things you can do. Often, a child may be resistant to potty training because it feels as if they're giving up control of something. Offering them control in other areas of their life could potentially help; i.e., allowing them to choose which TV show they'd like to watch, letting them pick their snacks or sides at dinner, etc.

Sticker charts and incentives can help, as well as potentially having others in their life make suggestions about using the potty—a caregiver or family member's suggestion could work.

Patience and allowing them to decide when they're ready to potty train seem to be the most effective way to get it done.

Talk to Your Child

It seems like a no-brainer, but simply asking your child what's wrong might help. If they're unable to express what's wrong in a 30,000-foot-view-type way, you may have to break your questions down to be more specific: What scares you about using the potty? Can you show me? What would make it more fun?

If your child is less verbal, it might take a bit of coaching or suggesting, but they might want to draw which part of the process is scary or point it out to you. Is it pooping? Is it a painting on the wall in the bathroom? Is it the flushing noise?

Give Your Child the Control

You could try dealing with accidents with less, not more, micromanagement. Some toddlers learn best when given the space to figure it out, even if it takes a bit longer. For these children, don't focus so much on reminding them of having to go to the potty. Deal with a few "oopsies" and see if they're able to course-correct on their own. It could prove more effective than everything you and your partner have been attempting.

Start Small

I like to think of these as "micro-encouragements." Commend them for simply alerting you or even just walking into the bathroom. Every little step is a win. Hopefully they'll get excited with the accruing victories and want to build on them.

DEALING WITH REGRESSION

Potty-training regression can be described as frequent accidents that cause you to go back to diapers. It is very common, so if it happens, don't get upset.

The most important part about regression is attempting to figure out exactly why it's happening. It could be that your child was never properly potty trained to begin with. You have to think back and ask yourself, were they showing an interest, as well as all the telltale signs of a child who is ready to use the potty?

If the answer is yes, then perhaps something else is going on. Stress is one of the most common causes of regression. Is there a new sibling in the family? Are you and your partner fighting or separating?

Other causes could be health issues, distractions, or an overall fear of actually using the toilet.

Luckily, a majority of regressions are short-lived and corrected within a few days or weeks. A positive attitude, gentle encouragements, and the rewards systems we covered earlier are great ways to get back on track.

Know When to Ask for Help

It's tough to know exactly when the right time is to ask for help. Some of the best support that I've received over the years has come from our parents and peers who have gone through the potty-training process.

Each child trains differently and the chances are good that, when asking friends and family about the subject, you're going to find similar war stories, with varying solutions or results.

There are often parenting or potty-training groups online (Facebook, etc.) that are full of folks reaching out for help or suggestions on how to tackle certain hiccups. Consulting the American Academy of Pediatrics website can offer some free medical insight, but you could also research experts in the field within your community. As with sleep-training and a myriad of other parenting milestones, people have created successful businesses in potty-training toddlers.

Any outstanding health symptoms obviously require the immediate attention of a physician, pediatrician, or urologist. They're also a dependable resource if you feel as if your child is reaching an older age and you don't have the type of progression that you feel you should have. At the very least, they can help you eliminate any medical concerns.

INSIDE YOUR CHILD'S MIND

Success is one thing, but failure is another.

With success, you'll find your child building more and more self-confidence in other areas beyond potty training, and hopefully you'll be able to find freedom from the cost and burden of diapers.

With failure, as I've mentioned, patience is the key throughout this entire process—not to mention parenting as a whole. Children generally want to make their parents happy, but sometimes the stress or fear becomes overwhelming and you'll experience slips or regression. Just remember to maintain a positive and encouraging attitude and never punish or degrade your children for having accidents. They're really just that: accidents.

CHEAT SHEET

1. **CONQUER NAPTIME FIRST.** This puts you closer to being able to achieve nighttime dryness.
2. **NIGHTTIME TRAINING IS DIFFICULT.** Accept that it could take months or possibly years before your child stops having accidents at night. Focus on being proactive and supportive instead.
3. **REGRESSION IS COMMON.** You didn't fail if this happens, but you need to identify why it's happening and work to address it. Think about changes, transitions, and other stressors.
4. **CONSTIPATION IS COMMON, TOO.** Fortunately, its generally solved with a dietary shift.
5. **PATIENCE AND POSITIVITY ARE STILL YOUR BEST TOOLS.**

Conclusion

Potty training during the daytime hours is hard enough, and once you've finally got that down, you face the challenges of making it through naptime and nighttime dry. Many of you will encounter bumps in the road, whether it be medical issues or natural forms of regression.

Eventually, you'll find success with your little one, but you can't stay at home forever. You'll need to consider a plan for successful bathroom practices outside of the home.

CHAPTER 7

Planes, Trains, and Automobiles

You should be proud you've made it this far and achieved a successful level of potty training at home. This is a major feather in your cap!

You've got a vocabulary and dialogue with your child, an established daily routine anchored in familiarity, as well as the equipment or additional accessories that you've acquired.

Not to take anything away from what you've got in the "win" column, but generally speaking, every team plays better when they're in their home stadium.

This chapter covers taking your team on the road and how to prepare yourself for different scenarios.

How to Prepare for Potty Training Outside the Home

Going anywhere, much less traveling the first week with a potty-training toddler, is a considerable challenge. It's certainly doable, but can also prove to be fairly miserable if you're not ready for it. So make sure to always have a backup plan, including having a portable potty and extra clothes and diapers.

In the early stages of potty training, if I needed to leave the house for whatever reason, I always made sure to limit fluid or food intake for about 30 minutes before we left. I would then walk my children to the bathroom and suggest that "we should try and go potty" before our trip, even if they said they didn't need to go. I'd often go so far as showing them that I was also going to "give it a try," even though I may not have needed to go, either.

If it was going to take us several minutes or more between the house and our destination, and I heard the dreaded "Daddy, I've gotta go pee-pee," I had the emergency potty in the back of our SUV. I could always pull over, assemble it, and avoid an accident in the car seat.

If our child did have an accident at our destination, I kept backup diapers in my backpack with an extra set of clothes or two, along with making sure I still had a healthy supply of wipes for cleaning up the situation.

The best thing that I can tell you is that you need to prepare to be unprepared and expect, not just the unexpected, but the unexpected dipped in a hot fart. If you can release the ideas of anything going smoothly, you'll be halfway there.

Childcare/Daycare

If you're a working parent, or just a parent who needs to enlist the help of some form of childcare or daycare, there are certain things to take into consideration.

Many childcare and daycare facilities these days mandate an age at which children must be potty trained and free of diapers. This is definitely something that you'll need to keep in mind while shopping around. Knowing this before you need to employ daycare services allows you the lead time to come up with a potty-training plan at home. Give yourself extra time for a margin of error.

With daycare services, it's often not the decision of the caregivers or even the administration that mandate ages of potty training. They do so because of licensing issues, legal concerns, or rules that can be beyond their control. There's a chance that you MIGHT be forced to change daycares in the event that your child isn't potty training and guess what? THAT. IS. OKAY. Better to find a new childcare solution than force your toddler into something they aren't ready for. No need to encourage the chance of regression.

If you've successfully potty trained your little one and are introducing them to daycare or childcare, you may want to speak with the caregiver about the opportunity to get the lay of the land with your toddler. Your child can experience the new bathroom setting with the comfort of you by their side, which could ultimately make for an easier and potentially flawless transition.

Playdates

You don't show up at playdates without pants on, and neither should your children. If you're doing the "no pants/naked" method of potty training, best practice might be to wait on playdates (unless you have close friends who don't mind the chance of a random turd or puddle appearing somewhere in their house).

The way I'd approach playdates isn't much different from introducing my kids to a new bathroom at a childcare or daycare. I'd ask your friend to first show you which bathroom is best to use and if you didn't bring your own supplies, ask questions such as where the toilet paper or potty seat might be, and whether they have wipes or a means to clean up any potential accidents. There's nothing worse than having to fly out of your friend's bathroom covered in poop in the middle of a "situation," asking where you can find everything.

Once you're familiar with their setup, perhaps you can take your child for a walk to give them the tour and encourage them to come and find you if they feel the urge. But I wouldn't put the sole onus on them. It might make sense to set a recurring alarm on your phone or stay within earshot so that you can get up and check on them frequently. Kids at this age get distracted VERY easily and if they're having fun, they can be oblivious to the fact that their bladder or bowels have sent up an SOS flag.

Public Restrooms

I hate them. And that's all I have to say about that. Kidding . . . but not really. I'm not sure that I could tell you the last time I pooped in a public restroom. Even when it's just to urinate, I play a little game with myself called "how few things can I touch in this bathroom?"

1. **Hands:** If I need to use a public restroom with a child (potty trained or not), I generally ask them to put their hands in their pockets. If that's not possible, I have them cross their arms. I tell them that I'll do a majority of the touching things, such as opening doors and acquiring soap, towels, etc.

2. **Knees:** Once you help them get on the big toilet, show them how to place their hands neatly on their knees. I began practicing this with them at home so that it translated to other places down the line. Don't despair if they can't grasp this concept right away; it takes a good amount of core balance and coordination to pull it off.

3. **Toes:** Once it comes time to wipe, I suggest helping them down or allowing your child to hop down OFF the potty. Have them bend over and touch their toes, but by all means DO NOT LET THEM TOUCH THE FLOOR. Sorry, am I coming off a bit too obsessive?

Toddlers love to grab the undersides of toilet seats, sides of the bowl, reach out for the gas station urinal boogie wall, or grab the soles of their shoes, so be vigilant, be specific, and help them. Places like the public library, large restaurants, airports, airplanes, etc. were designed with adults in mind, not necessarily small children.

Prepare your toddler before hitting the flusher or throwing your hands under the hand dryer—you might be surprised how loud and frightening these can be for a toddler—by giving them a warning and demonstrating how it's done. If they see you come out unscathed, they might have less of a problem doing it themselves.

Other Caregivers

Hiring in-home care offers a bit more flexibility than some of the larger childcare or daycare operations. It likely goes without saying, but finding a caregiver not only that you like, but that your child also likes and trusts, is of paramount importance. This thought is amplified if the caregiver is responsible for potty training, jumping in during the middle of your progress, or helping to continue your winning streak.

To provide a caregiver with the greatest chance of success, a well-organized list of what your child needs and has come to expect is paramount. This can include documenting the process by which you've potty trained your child, a quick list of nicknames or words your kid uses to indicate they have to use the restroom, and also the equipment or accessories that allow them to do it successfully.

Be sure to answer questions such as does the child like to wipe themselves or are they not capable? Is your family scrunchers or folders? Are there any rituals or fun songs that you do upon completion? What's the completion process look like? What is your handwashing/hygiene regimen? Do they get a sticker or reward for a job well-done?

I have to say, if I were the one taking care of your child, these are sacred CliffsNotes on how to ace the test.

Family and Friends

Family is a tricky one. If you happen to be dropping your kids off with your parents or the in-laws so you can have a much-needed date night, here are some things to keep in mind.

ASK NICELY. It might behoove you to pick up the phone and have a quick conversation with your family members before showing up with your kids. It could be a simple reminder to keep the toilet seats down (because little Johnny parks his Matchbox cars in there sometimes), a request to remove any sharp, dangerous, or valued vintage family heirlooms from the immediate toilet area, or a plea for them to keep their cool if an accident happens.

GET ON THE SAME PAGE. Often grandparents will want to revert to the way that they taught their kids (including yourself) and that may not mesh with the approach you've been taking. You might not need to hand over your caregiver toilet bible, but a few words about what your child is used to can't hurt.

Friends, on the other hand, especially close ones who may have children themselves, might have a greater sense of respect for the potty-training techniques and processes that you're trying to adhere to.

As with any place where you might be hanging out or dropping your kid off, it's always important to take a quick look at the environment. Will my child have access to everything they need so that we can avoid calling in a hazmat team after an afternoon poopie? Are there any inherent dangers, like open prescription pill bottles or a toilet seat that is too big for your little one's rear end? Are there decorative Japanese swords mounted on the wall within reach, or is there a bidet? Getting prepared ahead of your visit can avert potential problems.

COMMUNICATING WITH YOUR PARTNER

You have to keep in mind that if you're married or have a partner with whom you parent a child, you each grew up in different environments, with different methods of education.

It's difficult to always know what the other is thinking, but that's even more of a reason to sit down together and to come up with a plan. Read books and magazine articles, search online forums on social media, and talk to peers who might be going through (or have already gone through) the process with their own kids. Ask yourself, what is your division of labor? Do certain kids like being escorted to the bathroom by certain parents? Bring your ideas to the (dining-room) table and get together on what feels right—and stick to it (though do revisit it if there are hiccups).

In the Car

Remember when I said there were two things I'd never do? One was to get a minivan. (Nothing against minivan owners; they're just not my speed.) The other thing I said I'd never do is to have a toilet in my vehicle.

Let's just say that I'm batting .500 and I never bought a minivan.

We were given a foldable car potty when my wife was pregnant with our fourth child. It's quite sleek, I must say—it has its own carrying case that looks like a messenger bag. You can set it up in 30 seconds, allowing your child to pee or poop into bags, which are then sealed, enabling you to go on your way. This device has been a lifesaver.

Another fancy gadget we have is an accordion urinal for the boys (we call it "the frog" because of the adorable frog head on the lid). Now that our girls are older, we also have a female apparatus (don't ask me how this really works) that allows girls to pee into empty bottles.

Remember, there will be a myriad of times when a restroom is not available, because you are either in traffic, stuck in a snowstorm, at a ball field, waiting in a car line, or on some desolate stretch of road where bathroom access isn't just limited, it's nonexistent. These purchases have saved us time and time again.

On an Airplane or Train

Let's just be honest; airplane and train bathrooms are terrifying places for adults, let alone little kids. They're usually obscenely tiny, with a loud suctioning flush, bad water-flow in the sink, and nasty germs everywhere you turn. And that's not counting turbulence or bumping and shifting in the middle of trying to focus or aim. If it's this bad for adults, just imagine how difficult it can be for kids.

We were fortunate enough to avoid this type of travel while any of our four kids were potty training. However, we have traveled before and after and a lot of the same tactics apply.

When we travel with our gang, we make an effort to get to an airport or station with some time to spare. Once I wrangle two dollies of luggage and our four kids through security, we make an effort to find a family bathroom, which generally has benches, a changing table, and simply more room and privacy to do what you need to do. We get everyone to use the bathroom once before boarding and, once we're in the air or have had drink service and a snack, we usually take turns escorting each child to the bathroom. The alternative is to watch for signs and signals, which is easy when you've only got one child, but when there are multiples, it becomes increasingly difficult, hence the scheduled march to the potty.

Also, it's never a bad idea to travel with a pull-up on even if your child has graduated from that stage. Accidents happen and the last thing you want while traveling is contending with and trying to calm a wet, miserable child.

NOT THE MILE-HIGH CLUB YOU'VE HEARD ABOUT

This particular incident happened only once, but I have found myself in an air-travel situation in which I wasn't sure what to do.

My wife and I had just recently potty trained our daughter and were on a cross-country flight from Los Angeles to Philadelphia. Our daughter signaled to me that she needed to use the potty and my wife was holding our brand-new baby boy.

I rushed our daughter to the back of the plane and, once there, realized that both bathrooms were occupied. As I stood there, my panic began to grow. My daughter also grew more and more anxious, so I explained my situation to the flight attendant who gave a few tentative knocks to both bathroom doors, to no avail. The end result was that my daughter had an accident and there was really nothing I could do to prevent it, short of kicking in the door, which I'm sure wouldn't have been FAA-approved.

I always carried a gallon zip-top bag with an extra outfit for each of the kids in my backpack and this came in handy. I pulled it from overhead storage and finally dealt with our problem once one of the bathrooms opened up. I explained to my child that this was NOT her fault; sometimes accidents happen; no one else on the plane noticed (so she wouldn't be self-conscious), and we could just put it behind us—no need to focus more time or energy on it.

Emergency Situations

Emergencies can pop up for both you and your child.

If you're in the middle of potty training and something requires your immediate attention, do your best to stick to the routine. Lapses in continuity can cause mixed signals. Lean on a partner or family member for help, but by all means, if there just isn't a way to devote the time necessary into making this attempt work right then, don't be afraid to dial back and revert to the diaper. Wait until things calm down and ramp up another attempt!

In the sense of being a kid, emergencies will and do happen often. Bladder and bowel control take time and maturity. When I'm driving, one of my sons has a knack of telling me that he has to pee about 17 seconds before the dam breaks, which causes me to panic and possibly compromise my driving excellence so that he doesn't end with wet pants and I don't end up with a wet leather interior.

Emergencies in either capacity are going to happen. It's all part of the game. If there's one common through-line in this book, it's to keep your cool, stay patient, and be positive. You'll get through it!

AVOID COMPETITIVE PLAYDATES

Watch the competitive edge when it comes to playdates.

Parents often set up playdates with children of or around the same age. The reason that we do that is because, generally, their children are hitting the same or somewhat similar developmental milestones that our children are. The kids enjoy being together as they learn new words, games, and dances, and share new interests.

In the very beginning of this book, I emphasized the fact that not all kids are the same. It's been well documented that girls tend to potty train before boys, and not every child of a specific sex is ready at the same time.

One reason to keep this in mind is that, if you're hosting or attending a playdate, try to anticipate what you might need to have on hand OR what you might need to bring for an away game.

One more thing to remember is to be cognizant of another parent's feelings if their child isn't as far along as yours, so no need to become braggadocious. Also, don't accept pressure from another parent if your child isn't showing signs of being ready to potty train. Hold each other up, fellow parents!

CHEAT SHEET

1. **MAINTAIN YOUR POTTY-TRAINING MENTALITY.** Always have a plan when leaving the house with your little one. If they need to GO and you're in transit, at a friend's house, or in a public setting, what's your move?

2. **LEARN THE RULES.** If you're considering any form of childcare or daycare outside of the home, ask what their policy is on potty training. You may be required to have potty training done before admittance.

3. **PREPARE FOR PUBLIC BATHROOMS.** Navigating public restrooms can be a nightmare with toddlers. Create a routine that keeps hygiene on the forefront.

4. **TELL PEOPLE WHAT YOU NEED.** Get your family and friends on board. Share your potty-training process and encourage them to back you and any partner up by using positive reinforcement.

5. **PLANE, TRAINS, AND AUTOMOBILES.** Each one offers a different challenge. Think ahead and find the process that works best for you so as to avoid accidents.

Conclusion

Hopefully, I've been able to identify some potential challenges that you might face when leaving the house after beginning your potty-training journey—as well as some ideas and solutions to help you navigate problems via air, land, and sea.

Every child's and every parent's journey through potty training is different, but in the next section, I'll answer some of the most frequent questions.

PART IV

REAL-WORLD POTTY-TRAINING Q&A

While writing this book, I made a conscious effort to try and address mental preparation, reading your child's cues, finding a vocabulary and routine, and trouble-shooting snags that you may hit along the way.

We've talked about the importance of communicating with not only your child, but family members as well, to give potty training the greatest chances of success.

We discussed different methods of potty training and the importance of getting a win at home before venturing out to playdates or to go on a well-deserved vacation. But it's tough to know what each parent is experiencing, as each potty-training endeavor can be different.

Social media is good for a lot of things, like inflaming familial relations over politics, or dad-shaming someone wearing a baby carrier the wrong way, but one thing it is good for is sourcing opinions and ideas about children's developmental milestones.

Below, I've researched and also crowdsourced among my own followers on my parenting platform, *Dad or Alive*, some of the most commonly (and uncommonly) asked questions with what I hope are some helpful responses. Here are some questions from parents at large.

One of my biggest struggles has been teaching my little ones how to wipe properly. We've tried everything: Balloons with shaving cream, walking them through the process on dolls, standing over them and guiding their hand. Lord help me, I don't want these kids to go to college with skidmarks. What should I do?

This has been the source of much contention on my Facebook page. For 45 years, I thought that people only wiped one way; however, in a recent crowdsourcing expedition, I tossed the question out to my audience. The responses that I got were pretty surprising.

I asked my followers first, whether they FOLDED or SCRUNCHED.

I received an overwhelming response from people who didn't think they had time to "fold" and went for the quick scrunch or the "wrap it around your hand" wadding technique.

Then I asked them: Do you go between your legs and push front to back or do you do the "hook around" from front to back? This is extremely important for women so they can avoid urinary tract infections and to keep their other parts free of fecal matter.

Not that anyone is writing home about this, but I actually go between my legs, back to front with a certain cut-off point. I was blown away by the number of men AND women who wipe front to back and do the "hook around." It was mind-blowing. And we won't even get into those who responded that they stand to wipe.

So, keep in mind that technique can vary for everyone.

Anyway, back to our original question. Once you establish the technique that you want to teach, practice makes perfect. If using a doll or superhero figure to demonstrate isn't working, you might also consider a "dry run" with clothes on—mimic the action until they begin to understand. And remind them that they may need to wipe more than once!

Why oh why will my very intelligent three-and-a-half-year-old not poop on the toilet?

At three and a half the hope is that this child would be comfortable, but that's not always the case. You've got to get to the root of why they are avoiding the process. Was there a proper introduction to the toilet and what it does? Are they afraid of the flushing mechanism? If this is the case, perhaps take it in two steps. Ask them to go potty, and you'll take care of the flushing aspect afterwards and show them that it's nothing to be fearful of. Perhaps they're afraid of the size of an adult toilet and potentially falling in? If you think that's it, I would revert to a kid-size version so their feet are firmly planted on the ground and they don't feel as if they may get sucked into an unknown abyss, never to be seen again.

Why is there so much pressure on parents to potty train by a certain age?

That's a great question and the answer is: There shouldn't be. To each their own. Most children will begin to shows signs of being ready to potty train between the ages of 18 to 24 months; however, some kids may not show these signals until they're three years old. I wouldn't allow social peer pressures to dictate your child's progress.

If you are personally getting sick of buying and changing diapers, you can always gently begin to make suggestions to your child or even try to put them on the potty. You'll know pretty fast if your child is ready to start training or not.

Why is it important to start potty training a boy sitting down? I had the hardest time with this and one day my son told me that he just wanted to stand, took aim, and never looked back.

There is no definitive answer to this. Again, the older your child is, the easier it might be to potty train a boy to pee standing up first. It always made the most sense for us to start boys or girls sitting down. They both need to sit to have a bowel movement, and sitting proved to be the easier and most effective way to begin.

They were both able to pee and poop in that position. After they mastered that action, they began to become curious about why I stood up to urinate. Once they began to show that interest, that was when we began to work on technique. Young boys tend to have not only bad aim but also a very short attention span. I often found them hosing off the walls and floors—almost everything *but* the toilet.

Once you've conquered sitting down and peeing and pooping, how do you transition your boys to stand up to pee?

Great question! After our boys had successfully learned how to pee and poop on the potty sitting down, they began to show interest and ask why Daddy peed standing up. I tried to explain to them that sometimes I have to pee and not poop and it's a little quicker to pull the front of your pants down or use your zipper rather than undoing a belt and buttons and getting partially undressed.

I've heard of a few different ways to work on aim. Cereal seems to be the top contender—placing some sort of O's or cereal ring in the water and allowing them to aim for it and hit it until they're done. Another method I've heard of, but not seen yet, is to paint a red "X" on the bottom of the toilet bowl— whether this be with lipstick or some other non-permanent method, but it allows them to take aim at a stationary object instead of chasing the cereal around the bowl. The third way that I just recently heard about via a Facebook follower was to allow them to pee in a soup can outside—the boy thought it was fun and this fan said her son was trained to aim in five days.

I bought my daughter a doll that came with her own potty and she was very excited to start potty training; unfortunately, my daughter now wants to use the doll's potty instead of her own. Is this common?

I'd be lying if I said that you're the first to experience this. Our youngest, Evelyn, has (more than once) attempted to sit on a doll toilet and go potty. Thankfully she never got undressed or actually went to the bathroom—evidently it was merely to show me how dolly went potty.

Should I keep using diapers or pull-ups or go straight to underwear?

As I mentioned earlier in this book, we chose to do the "stay home for a week and go naked from the waist down" technique. After those five or six days, I switched to underwear. I may have used a pull-up for naptime and overnight, but did my best to limit the child's fluid and food intake for about 30 to 60 minutes before they lay down. I encouraged them to continue alerting me if they had to use the potty and celebrated with them if they woke up dry.

I was always afraid that putting them back in diapers or pull-ups while potty training was going to confuse the message I was trying to give them. They had found comfort in peeing and pooping in a diaper/pull-up all this time, so having that feeling of being in them might feel like it was okay to have accidents . . .

My child has potty trained successfully during the daytime hours, but can't make it through the night without wetting the bed. What should I do?

Don't fret. Most kids will successfully daytime potty train and wear underwear by three or so years old. Nighttime training might come months or even years after that. Some pediatricians even recommend waiting until your child is five years of age before giving that a go.

You can certainly try earlier, but I would first limit the fluid/food intake approximately 30 to 60 minutes before bed and consider buying a plastic or water-resistant fitted sheet that can go under their mattress, so as not to ruin it. Prepare yourself for a LOT of soiled pajamas and sheets.

What should I do if my toddler isn't really getting potty training or is hating the process?

Even if your toddler has shown the interest and basic signs and signals, they just might not be ready to embrace the process. Every motion and action involved with potty training is a piece to a puzzle. If you can't put the pieces together, you won't get a finished product. My suggestion is to pull back for a few weeks and give it another shot then.

My toddler throws a tantrum every time we have to use a public restroom. He's fine without his diapers at home, but he has a real fear of using a bathroom that is new to him. What can I do?

It seems like there are two solutions to this problem. The first would be to show your toddler by example that it's safe and okay to use the public restroom. Watching you use the toilet might make it okay for them to give it a shot as well. Don't be afraid to walk through the entire process with them, including showing them the flusher, where to get the toilet paper, etc. and letting them know that you're not leaving their side.

The other solution if the situation is completely unmanageable would be to offer them the ability to go out to the car and use the car potty—if that's even an option. It may not be the most convenient, but it could help to avert an accident in a restaurant or retail store when you really don't have time to deal with it.

Is it okay for my child to use a regular-size adult toilet to potty train?

If your child is big enough to use an adult-sized toilet without falling into the center of the Earth or is free of any fear, then there's really nothing wrong with it. In my experience, it's always seemed much easier to get them their own miniature version or, at the very least, some sort of insert that reduces the size of the toilet-seat hole. These days, there are some very nice replacement seats that have a child option that snaps into place and can be removed when company comes over. They match the aesthetic of a regular white bowl and look no different.

Is "poop training" different from regular potty training?

Being able to sit down on the potty and go pee is one of the easier parts of potty training. You may have a child who is hesitant to go poop in the potty, and will only poop in a pull-up. It's fine to let them continue to do that; however, each time it happens, walk them to the toilet and allow them to see you put the poop from the Pull-up into the toilet. Tell them that "that's where the poop goes." After a few times, they may understand better what you want from them.

You can also make an attempt to get them a small footstool so that they're able to "bear down," making bowel movements easier to release.

With a new sibling on the way, should we stop potty training our three year old? I'm afraid she might regress.

Personally, I would stay the course. You and your partner are going to have your hands full with a newborn and may not have the time or energy to begin potty training after you get home from the hospital.

If you're relying on friends and family to help out during the birth and recovery process, perhaps consider writing up a one-page instructional that notes how you've been potty training her. Include a short list of any nicknames for things, the process you've been adhering to, as well as any kind of post-potty ritual/celebration/song or reward chart that you've established.

Are there different methods for potty training boys versus girls?

We potty trained our two boys and two girls sitting down. Shortly after learning how to pee and poop sitting down, our boys showed interest and graduated to standing up to urinate. The big red flag here is mainly with girls and technique. Girls need to be wiped from front to back to avoid bacteria getting into sensitive areas and causing urinary tract infections.

A Final Note

Congratulations, Dad! Hopefully you made it all the way through this book AND the potty training process. It's my sincere hope that you were able to wrap your head around this endeavor and see it from start to finish, and everything in between.

I hope that you've found the strategies I laid out helpful and made adjustments along the way that fit your child's personality and developmental progress.

There are so many milestones to celebrate with your child in these younger years and for me, this was always one of the toughest to achieve. It sometimes takes an incredible amount of patience and perseverance (two things I've admittedly lacked through the years) to find the finish line and, even then, you still might have an accident or two.

You may find yourself dashing out of restaurants, cleaning up messes in the movie theater restroom, pulling off the freeway in a scramble to find a public bathroom, or assembling the potty in the back of your car, but the KEY is to stay calm and be able to pivot. This too shall pass. And your child will eventually be not just proud, but happy, to be diaper-free and living that clean underwear life!

All the best,
Adrian

Resources

BusyToddler.com

Website run by an early childhood education advocate and former teacher with great insights.

ClevelandClinic.org

A nonprofit academic medical center that provides education and health information.

DadOrAlive.com

Adrian Kulp's personal parenting blog, documenting stories on raising four young kids with a good dose of humor.

Fatherhood.org

The National Fatherhood Initiative is a nonprofit focused on eliminating or reducing father absence.

Fathers.com

A nonprofit organization that provides encouragement, support, and guidance for fathers.

GetParentingTips.com

Offers resources to help parents, caregivers, childcare providers, community members, companies, and organizations give our children a better upbringing.

HiMyNameIsMom.com

Podcast from real moms that offer real-world parenting insights.

KidsHealth.org

The number-one most-trusted source for physician-reviewed information and advice on children's health and parenting issues.

LifeOfDad.com

The largest online fatherhood community, offering access to millions of dads across the globe.

LifeOfMom.com

Motherhood community offering access to moms across the globe as well as important parenting insights.

MayoClinic.org

Nonprofit medical center that provides education and research.

NIH.gov

Medical research agency that supports turning scientific discoveries into healthy practices.

Pampers.com

Run by the maker of Pampers, this site has a wealth of information on pregnancy, baby care, and parenting tips.

Parents.com

A monthly magazine that features scientific information on child development.

PsychologyToday.com

Website providing everything from behavioral research to practical guidance on various subjects.

VeryWellFamily.com

Provider of facts on kids' health and helpful parenting tips.

WhatToExpect.com

Information on baby and toddler development.

References

Brucks, Brandi. *Potty Training in Three Days: The Step-by-Step Plan for a Clean Break from Dirty Diapers.* Emeryville, CA: Althea Press, 2016.

"Busy Toddler—Making It to Naps, One Activity at a Time." 2021. Busy Toddler. Accessed March 4, 2021. busytoddler.com.

Glowacki, Jamie. *Oh Crap! Potty Training: Everything Modern Parents Need to Know to Do It Once and Do It Right.* New York: Gallery Books, 2015.

Mayo Clinic Staff. "Potty Training: How to Get the Job Done." Mayo Clinic. October 5, 2019. mayoclinic.org/healthy-lifestyle /infant-and-toddler-health/in-depth/potty-training/art-20045230.

McCoy, Jazmine. *The First-Time Parent's Guide to Potty Training: How to Ditch Diapers Fast (and for Good!).* New York: Zeitgeist, 2020.

National Institute of Diabetes and Digestive and Kidney Diseases. "Eating, Diet, & Nutrition for Constipation in Children." Last modified May 2018. niddk.nih.gov/health-information/digestive-diseases /constipation-children/eating-diet-nutrition.

Swaney, Michelle D. *The Complete Guide to Potty Training: The Step-by-Step Plan with Expert Solutions for Any Mess.* Emeryville, CA: Althea Press, 2018.

Vethavanam, Vido. "Potty Training: The Truth." MadeForMums. Accessed March 11, 2021. madeformums.com/toddler-and-preschool /potty-training-the-truth.

Index

Acknowledgments

Without my wife, Jen, and our four beautiful children, Ava, Charlie, Mason, and Evelyn, I never would have written this book.

Jen and I have washed soiled sheets, dealt with exploded diapers, dried toddler pants using the truck's heater, and removed several (are you kidding me?!) potty-training seats from around the neck of our son Charlie. I wouldn't trade any of those curse-word-fueled moments for anything.

Thanks to my parents, Bruce and Joan, for teaching me how to "fold," not "scrunch" . . .

A big thanks to my in-laws, Bob and Elaine, (for sneaking M&Ms as poopy treats), as well as extended family on both sides, for helping us navigate many a middle-of-the-night accident.

About the Author

Adrian Kulp has worked as a comedy booking agent for CBS, a TV executive for Adam Sandler's Happy Madison Productions, and as a vice president of development for Chelsea Handler's Borderline Amazing Productions.

For the past 11 years, he's been the voice behind the popular dad blog *Dad or Alive: Confessions of an Unexpected Stay-at-Home Dad*, which was published as a comedic memoir in 2013, and he's also produced the reality series *Modern Dads* for A&E Networks.

In 2018, he penned his second book and bestseller, *We're Pregnant! The First-Time Dad's Pregnancy Handbook.* He has since written *We're Parents! The New Dad's Guide to Baby's First Year; We're Parenting a Toddler! The First-Time Parents' Guide to Surviving the Toddler Years;* and *World's Greatest Dad Jokes.*

He lives in Nashville, Tennessee, with his wife, Jen, and their four kids, Ava, Charlie, Mason, and Evelyn.

About the Illustrator

Jeremy Nguyen is an illustrator and cartoonist whose work regularly appears in the *New Yorker* magazine. He has worked with *Wired*, the *Nib*, *New York Magazine*, and HBOMax, among others. When he's not drawing, you can find him curled up with a good comic book and a hot cup of tea. He currently lives in Brooklyn, NY.